BROWSE

Magazine

Printed in the U.S.A.

ISBN 978-0-544-57909-5

2 3 4 5 6 7 8 9 10 0877 24 23 22 21 20 19 18 17 16 15

4500545608 A B C D E F G

Cover Photo Credits: ©Digital Vision/Getty Images

Houghton
Mifflin
Harcourt

hmhco.com

BROWSE
Magazine

UNIT 1

UNIT 1
Culture and Belonging
Language
Art
Subculture
Poetry

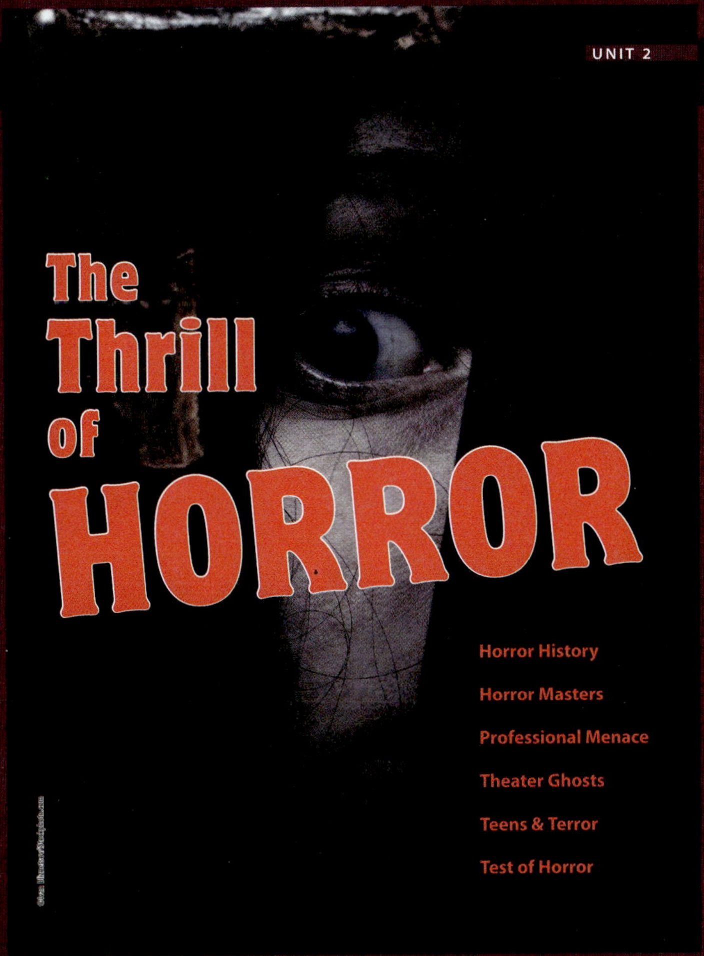

UNIT 2
The Thrill of HORROR
Horror History
Horror Masters
Professional Menace
Theater Ghosts
Teens & Terror
Test of Horror

UNIT 2

UNIT 3

UNIT 3
The Move Toward
FREEDOM
Women's Fashion, Women's Freedom
Open Air Zoos
Living Off the Grid
A Legendary Escape

UNIT 4
Approaching
Adulthood

UNIT 4

UNIT 5

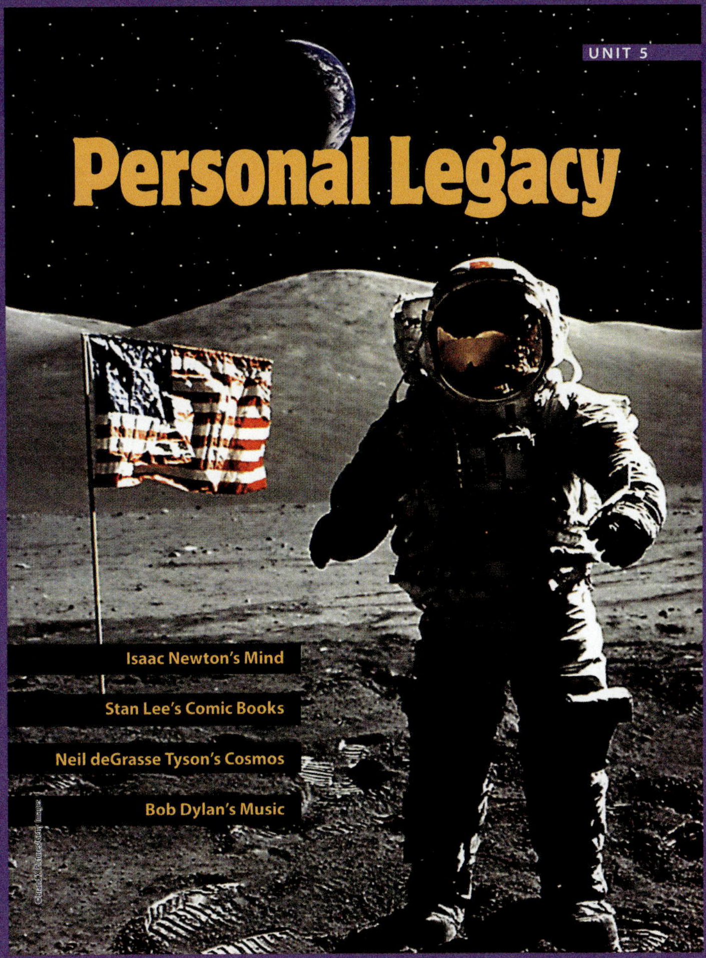

UNIT 5
Personal Legacy
Isaac Newton's Mind
Stan Lee's Comic Books
Neil deGrasse Tyson's Cosmos
Bob Dylan's Music

UNIT 6
The Value of Work
Work/Life Balance
Workplace Changes
Learn a Trade
Entrepreneur Earning
Work Riddles

UNIT 6

UNIT 1

Culture and Belonging

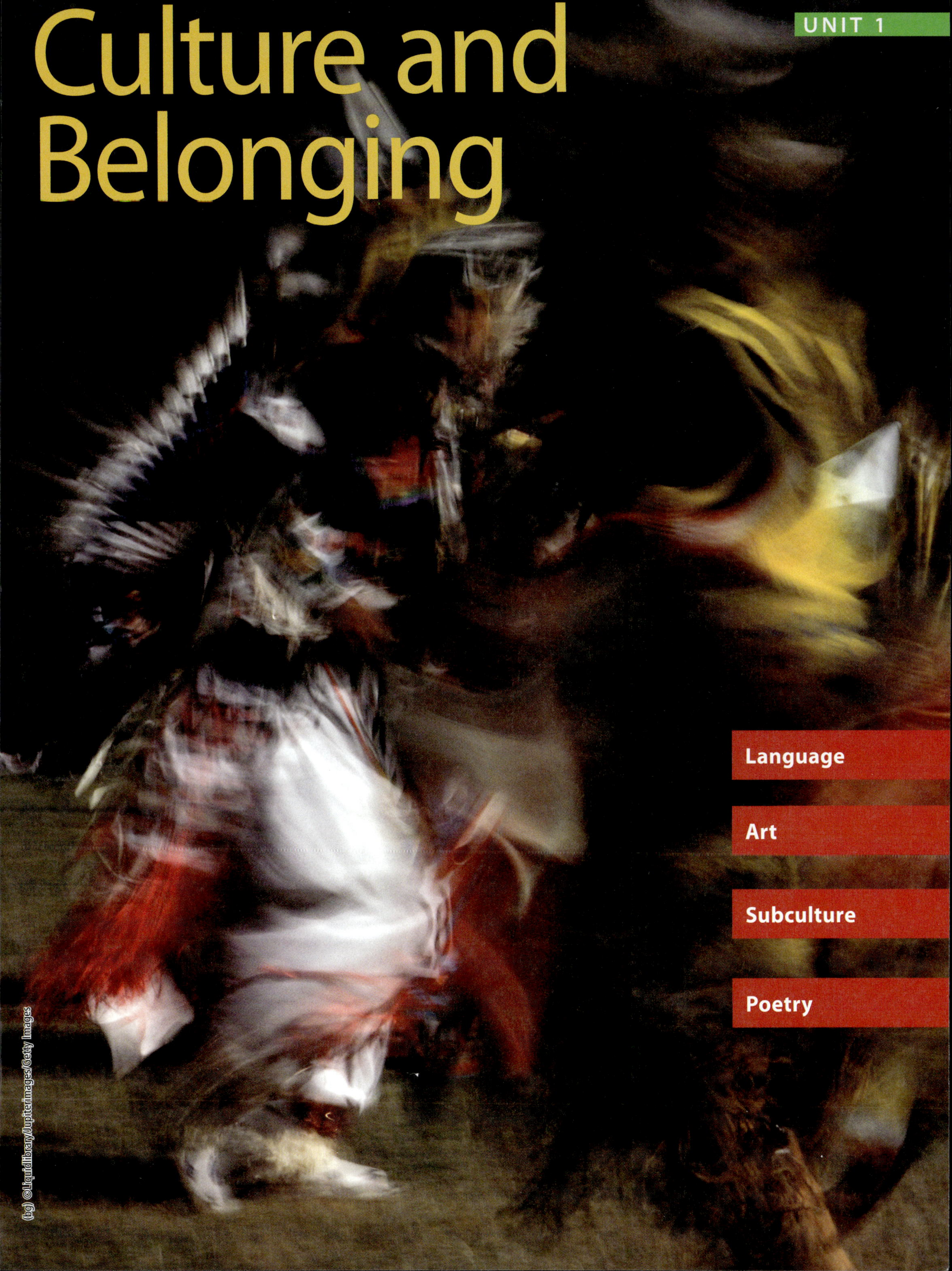

Language

Art

Subculture

Poetry

(bg) ©Liquidlibrary/Jupiterimages/Getty Images

Language and Culture

You're at a diner, and you order a sandwich made with a long roll of bread. If you're from New Jersey, you might ask for a submarine; if you're from Louisiana, you might ask for a poor boy. Or perhaps you're from Philadelphia, and you ask for a hoagie. Or you're a New Yorker, and you order a hero.

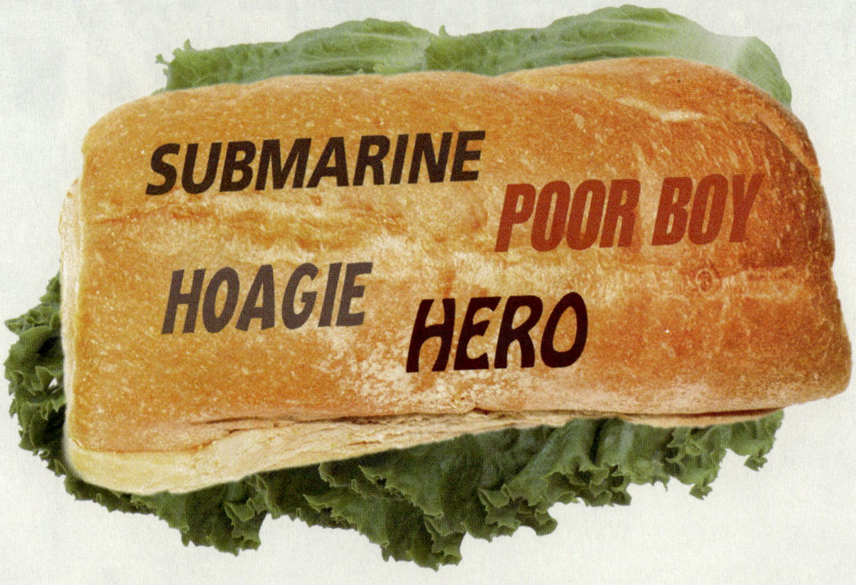

The name you use for a sandwich may reveal a little bit about yourself, but in a bigger sense, language is the main tool you use to express your culture—whether you know it or not! Your views are influenced by your culture, and the language you use to communicate them has been shaped by that culture.

(bg) ©Maksim Shmeljov/Shutterstock; (c) ©Houghton Mifflin Harcourt; (c) ©Liz Van Steenburgh/Shutterstock

So where and when did language start? There are no fossilized adjectives, no nouns trapped in lava, no concrete clues. Speech is just a puff of air and a sound that's gone as soon as it's made. (Writing came much later.) One theory is that all modern languages—about 6,000 of them—had a common origin: a single language spoken more than 50,000 years ago by early African humans.

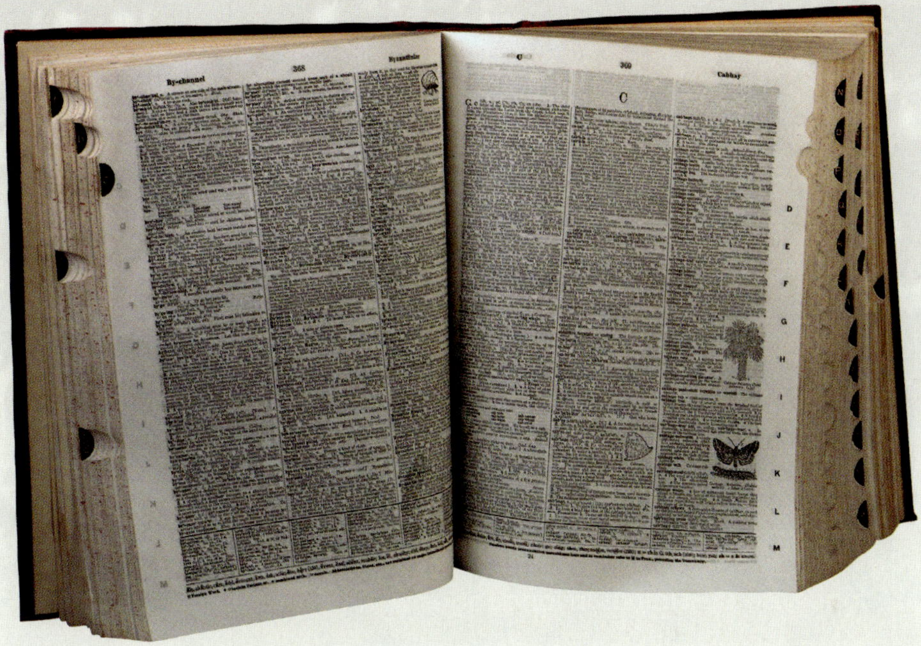

In English, we might start a sentence "Doctor Brown sat on a . . ." We use the past tense, *sat*. In Russian, you'd also use the past tense, but the verb form would differ for a male doctor and a female doctor. And in Turkish, the verb would let the listener know if you actually saw the doctor sitting or if you just heard or read about it.

Every language changes over time to reflect the culture of the people who use it. As humans spread from Africa around the world, six major language groups emerged. The Indo-European language group is spoken by half the world's population; it incudes languages as varied as English, Farsi, Hindi, Russian, and Spanish. Of course, each of these languages has itself changed. New vocabulary is needed to describe new inventions and our expanded understanding of the environment, and languages also change considerably when the nations that use them are invaded, colonized, or have significant numbers of immigrants. So language reflects culture in real time.

The tiny island of La Gomera lies off the northwest coast of Africa. It's a mountainous island with numerous deep ravines. The original inhabitants of La Gomera invented a unique language, which the Spanish settlers in the 1400s also adapted. The language is called Silbo Gomera, and it's all whistles! The tones rise and fall as in languages with words, but they have one huge advantage: the whistles carry for miles across the rugged landscape, and their messages reach the listeners intact. The island's local government worried that Silbo Gomera was dying out, so now it's a compulsory subject in school!

Some languages may share the same roots but sound completely different and still mirror their speakers' individual cultures. (Take Swedish and Celtic, for example.) A language is a common bond that its users share. But it would be a mistake to think that the limits of one's language limit one's understanding. People can have feelings and concepts that their language has no words for. (Look up the German word *Schadenfreude*.)

And if you don't understand what someone says, you can always respond the way they do in English, Italian, Mandarin, Spanish, Icelandic, Siwu, Lao, Dutch, Cha'palaa, and Murriny Patha. Just say, "Huh?"

ART on EARTH

Here on this planet, there's a great way to find out more about our various cultures through the ages: art. Art tells us a lot about the people who produced it and about the technology and skills of the time and place.

While art teaches us about other cultures, it can also teach us more about our own—our art reflects all parts of our culture. And art is often the most creative of a culture's achievements, and the best of it is treasured and passed down.

This cave painting is from Lascaux, France, and is over 17,000 years old. Stone Age people didn't have supermarkets—this painting lets us know they took hunting seriously!

Everyone knows that ancient Egyptians built pyramids and crafted amazing gold jewelry. This 3,500-year-old wall painting shows that music was important to them, too.

About 8,000 life-size soldiers—each with unique features—guard the tomb of China's first emperor. They were made of clay over 2,200 years ago. The tomb itself is the size of a football field, and remains unexplored. (It's hard to imagine what treasures might be hidden there.)

When Mount Vesuvius erupted nearly 2,000 years ago, the ancient Roman city of Pompeii was buried in ash. Much of the town was preserved. Here's a mosaic from the entrance to one of the houses. The words *cave canem* are Latin for "beware of the dog."

This Mayan pyramid at Palenque, Mexico, contained wonderful treasures. It's the tomb of K'inich Janaab' Pakal, who died in 683. His stone sarcophagus weighs 20 tons!

The Normans invaded England in 1066, and changed much of its culture forever. The Bayeux Tapestry, dating from that time, makes it clear that the knights didn't carry their own armor.

The kingdom of Benin in western Africa lasted from the 1200s through the 1800s, and was famous for its ivory and bronze art. This bronze casting shows a leopard—a symbol of royal power. It is said that in the 1600s, the Benin king was accompanied by tame leopards on chains when he walked though the city.

Painting turned a corner when J. M. W. Turner revolutionized landscape painting in the first half of the 1800s. Already a celebrated English artist, Turner used a new style to express the powers of nature and light. In this painting, he pays respect to the great warship *Temeraire* as it is towed off to be scrapped. The *Temeraire* had played a key role in the British had victory at the Battle of Trafalgar.

That's all the room there is here, but you can look on Internet for more

The Spanish architect Antoni Gaudi was a master interpreter of numerous styles, and in 1914 he completed Park Güell in Barcelona. The park isn't exactly a reflection of the culture of the time—it's more of an cxpansion of many parts of the culture mixed together playfully and brilliantly.

Afghanistan has had a rich tradition in art, literature, and music for thousands of years, and its carpets are world-renowned. Much of Afghanistan's cultural expression has suffered during the wars there. This rug was made during the Soviet war of the 1980s—it isn't very hard to see what was on the weaver's mind.

The East Side Gallery stretches for four-fifths of a mile along what's left of the Berlin Wall in Germany. The wall had been the symbol of the division of Europe. This is one place where graffiti is a welcome and admired part of the neighborhood!

information and images showing art from cultures through the ages.

sub culture

Sapeurs

For 80 years, the Republic of the Congo was ruled by the French. As in most colonies, life wasn't the same for the indigenous people as it was for those doing the colonizing. After independence in 1960, a social movement called *La Sape* took shape. It's short for *Société des Ambianceurs et des Personnes Élégantes* (the Society for the Advancement of Elegant People). As a statement of resistance, the members of this subculture outdo their former rulers in style and manners!

There are people who search outside traditional culture for a community where they feel they belong. Some do this out of a driving need—others have a strong enough safety net in their own society to feel safe "touring" a subculture.

The members of a subculture share common views and beliefs, while rejecting some of the values of the larger culture they exist in. However large the subculture, it becomes something of a substitute family in which common values are understood.

There's a lot of accepted mainstream culture that didn't start thay way. In the early twentieth century, most people didn't consider jazz to be music—and it was thought to endanger traditional values. (It's interesting to note that many classical composers faced similar reactions in their day.) Rock 'n' roll was belittled and hated, and so was hip-hop. It's possible that these reactions actually helped popularize these movements and draw the people involved closer together. People with new ideas in the arts, fashion, and literature often begin as outcasts, and they bond with others who are treated the same.

It may not take long for the larger culture to pick up on some of the ideas of a subculture and to identify its interesting and valuable contributions. Or maybe the subculture just seems much cooler than everything else! But when large numbers of people start to look and act as though they are in a particular subculture, the subculture moves on. Perhaps the adoption of their values is too superficial for the original members, or perhaps it becomes too commonplace to be cool anymore.

Punk music originated in the 1970s, abstract expressionist painting in the 1940s. Both movements have survived.

The Lone Wolf

Wolves normally live in packs. A wolf that has left the pack or has been driven away is called a *lone wolf* and lives independently.

Some people are described as lone wolves.

Yeah I've got a shadow
And that's all I've got.
I am my own company,
I can see in the dark.
It's where I live.

And I post no bills.
I'm not his or hers,
I'm not yours babe.
I don't belong to anyone.
I don't belong.

I'm off the beaten track,
off-line and off-key.
I'm off the hook,
offstage in the wings.
I'm on this flight.

I'm the what and where
on the horizon,
I'm the how of the blue.
I'm the card that's missing
from the pack.

I'm not in the fine print
or even on the page.
I don't need a reason,
I don't want to rhyme.
I can't — Lone Wolf.

Angel Island

Angel Island, the largest island in the San Francisco Bay, takes up just over one square mile of space. Between 1910 and 1940, about one million people passed through the island—it was the door to the United States for Asian immigrants. But the door was only half open.

The United States is an immigrant nation. Almost all the people living here have their roots in other parts of the world. It's part of this country's culture to welcome others to these shores. Usually.

Chinese immigrants began arriving in large numbers during the California Gold Rush of the mid 1800s. They then became a crucial part of the labor force as the western frontier was developed—but people resented the presence of the Chinese and argued that they would take employment from the existing population. For the first time in its history, the United States enacted a law to limit immigration—from China. In 1882, the Chinese Exclusion Act was passed, and remained in place until 1943 (when China became a U.S. ally in World War II).

Historic ruin at Angel Island National Historic Park

When immigrants reached Angel Island, they were detained in barracks while their paperwork was processed. A detainee might be held for days, months, even a year. Although most of the arrivals came from China, there were large numbers of Japanese, and also immigrants from Russia, Mexico, India, Korea, and the Philippines.

Chinese immigrants arrive at Angel Island

After World War II, Angel Island became a state park, and the immigration station was abandoned. It remained almost forgotten until a park ranger made a remarkable discovery: carved into the wooden walls of the barracks were hundreds of Chinese poems, written by those who had been held there years earlier.

This is a message to those who live here not to worry excessively.
Instead, you must cast your idle worries to the flowing stream.
Experiencing a little ordeal is not hardship.
Napoleon was once a prisoner on an island.

BADGES

There's an easy way to show what you value, what you're good at, or what you believe. Wear it! Badges are like flags—they show where you belong.

Use the clues to help you find the description and picture of of each badge. Some of the clues are pretty tricky! You may need to use the Internet for help.

Clues		Description		Badge	
A	Letters in naval semaphore signals are made by the position of flags held in each hand. They can be simplified into straight lines.	a	The emblem of Emergency Medical Services	1	
B	In 1991, a group of artists designed a simple symbol in a color that represents the heart and love.	b	A button representing balance	2	
C	Chinese philosophy states that contrasting forces—yin and yang—work together to make a whole.	c	Radiation danger—nobody wears this!	3	
D	Scientists designed a unique and striking symbol that might suggest the action of atomic particles.	d	A pin worn on Memorial Day	4	
E	The symbol of Asclepius, the ancient Greek god of medicine and healing, was a snake and a rod.	e	A button supporting nuclear disarmament	5	
F	The only flower that would grow in many destroyed battlefields in France in World War I was the poppy.	f	The symbol of AIDS awareness	6	

Now design your own badge to represent something that you value, believe in, or have achieved.

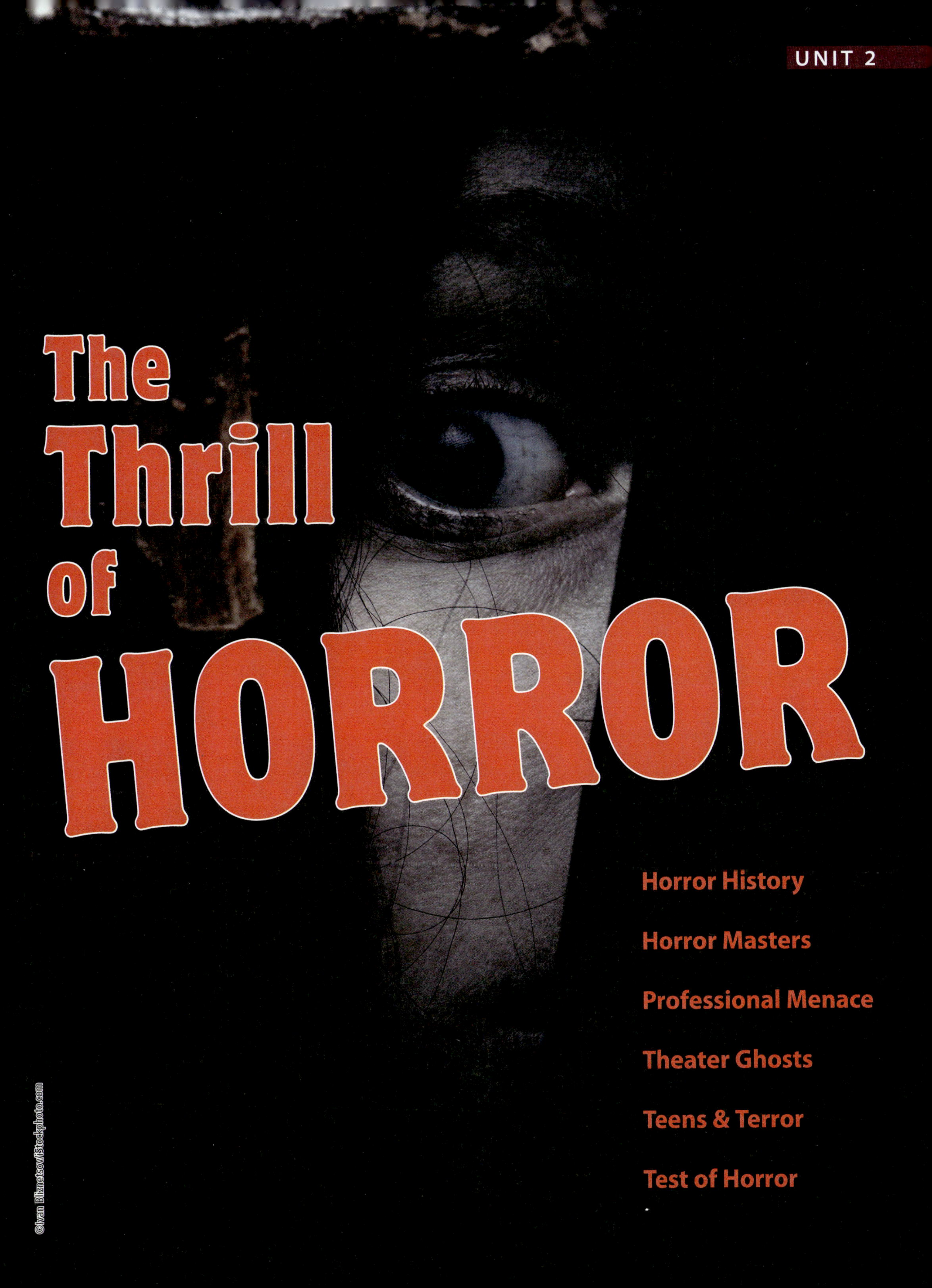

The Thrill of HORROR

Horror History

Horror Masters

Professional Menace

Theater Ghosts

Teens & Terror

Test of Horror

A Brief History of Horror

783 BCE Legend has it that in China, King Xuan of the Zhou Dynasty was killed by the ghost of his former minister, Tu Po, three years after Xuan had Po executed on false charges.

1st Century CE Pliny the Younger writes a letter where he relays a tale of a haunted house. The ghost of an old man terrorizes the residents of a house in Athens.

856 CE A farmhouse in Germany was thought to be haunted by a poltergeist (a German word that means "noisy spirit"), disturbing the residents by throwing stones, starting fires, and causing chaos.

1601 CE Shakespeare writes *Hamlet*, the story of a prince who sees the ghost of his father. The ghost tells Hamlet gruesome details of his death, haunting his son until he's driven him to madness.

1818 CE Mary Shelley publishes *Frankenstein*.

1825 CE In Japan, horror stories also come into vogue, with the very popular Kabuki play *Yotsuya Kaidan*, the tale of a man haunted by the ghost of his wife.

1845 CE Edgar Allan Poe writes his most famous work, "The Raven," published in *The Evening Mirror*.

1874 CE Composer Camille Saint-Saëns presents his orchestral poem, *Danse macabre*, about a personified Death calling forth the dead from their graves to dance for him on Halloween.

1896 CE Georges Méliès creates what is arguably the first horror film called *Le Manoir du diable* (*The Haunted Castle*). The film features many tropes of the horror genre on screen for the first time.

1897 CE Bram Stoker publishes *Dracula*.

1922 CE German film director F. W. Murnau releases one of the most influential horror films of all time, an adaptation of Bram Stoker's *Dracula* called *Nosferatu*.

1960 CE Alfred Hitchcock releases the classic thriller, *Psycho*.

1977 CE Stephen King writes *The Shining*. In 1980 the novel was adapted to a popular film directed by Stanley Kubrick and starring Jack Nicholson.

2006 CE Guillermo del Toro releases *Pan's Labyrinth*, a dark fantasy film that gains universal acclaim using elements of horror.

PRESENT DAY Horror as a genre continues to thrive through the continued production and popularity of spooky books, films, and video games.

Masters of

Alfred Hitchcock was a famous English film director, considered to be the "Master of Suspense," and one of the greatest filmmakers ever. His movies were famous for inducing anxiety, fear, and suspense. One of Hitchcock's most famous film, *Psycho* told the story of a secretary who steals money from her job so she can run away and marry her boyfriend. While fleeing town, she stops at the Bates Motel and meets the owner, who has the strange hobby of stuffing dead animals and an unusual relationship with his mother. The shower scene, in which a screaming woman is attacked with a kitchen knife, is one of film's most iconic images

H. P. Lovecraft was a famous American horror author. He was generally unknown during his lifetime, but became celebrated after his death. As a child, his father was confined to a mental institution and he was raised in part by his grandfather, who loved to tell stories. Lovecraft began composing elaborate horror tales as a child and continued to do so into his adult years. These tales focused on strange, ancient deities who existed outside human perception. One of these deities, Cthulhu, was described as a mix of man, octopus, and dragon—and the mere sight of this creature drove humans insane.

Horror

Stephen King is an American novelist who has published over 55 novels. He is known for stories in which average people, often from small towns, must fight great evil or overcome supernatural powers. His wife convinced him to publish his first novel, *Carrie*, after he tried to throw it away. *Carrie* is about a teenage girl who uses her psychokinetic powers, or ability to move things with her mind, to punish her cruel peers.

Edgar Allan Poe was a celebrated American writer, known for his tales of mystery and death. Poe had a tough life; he was orphaned as a child, lost his beloved wife to illness, and struggled with poverty. Poe's writing often features tales of death, premature burial, obsession, and grief. His most famous poem, "The Raven," depicts a man falling into madness after the death of his love. In "The Tell-Tale Heart," a murderer describes how he killed a man and buried him under the floor. The villain is slowly driven mad, hearing the mysterious beating of the heart of his victim.

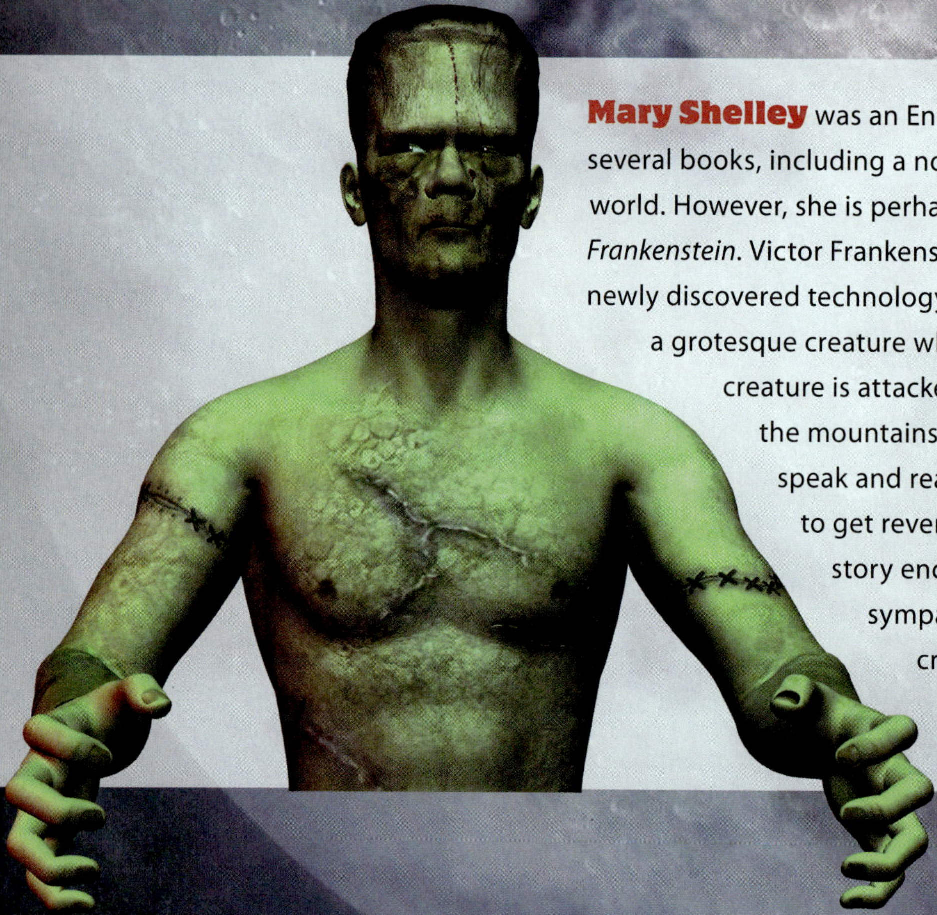

Mary Shelley was an English novelist, who wrote several books, including a novel about the end of the world. However, she is perhaps best known for writing *Frankenstein*. Victor Frankenstein, a scientist, uses the newly discovered technology of electricity to bring to life a grotesque creature who he then abandons. The creature is attacked by villagers and flees into the mountains. He teaches himself how to speak and read, then returns to civilization to get revenge on his creator. Shelley's story encourages the reader to sympathize with the "monster" and criticizes those who reject others for being different.

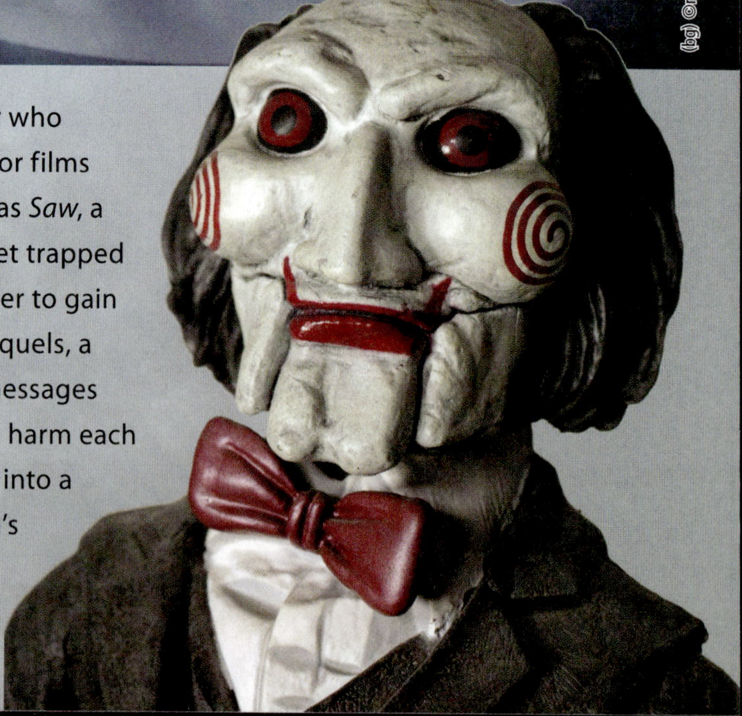

James Wan is an Australian filmmaker who created some of the most celebrated horror films in recent history. His first major success was *Saw*, a psychological thriller in which two men get trapped in a bathroom and must turn on each other to gain their freedom. Throughout *Saw*'s many sequels, a mysterious puppet named Billy delivers messages to captured victims, often forcing them to harm each other. In Wan's *Insidious*, a young boy falls into a coma and is taken over by evil spirits. Wan's style has been described as twisted and gory, and his plots are praised for their complexity.

(bg) ©najin/iStockphoto.com; (tl) ©YorkBerlin/Shutterstock; (br) ©Bornfree/Shutterstock

George A. Romero is an American filmmaker and is considered the king of zombie films. He started making films at age 14, and after college he directed film segments on *Mister Rogers' Neighborhood*. He and his friends produced and filmed *Night of the Living Dead* in 1968. This movie follows a brother and sister on a trip to the countryside where they're quickly attacked by zombies. The zombie assault is violent and seemingly unstoppable. Romero then made *Dawn of the Dead*, a film in which zombies have again overrun America and a group of civilians is forced to fight for their lives, while they are trapped in a shopping mall. Romero's films are known for their gore, violence, and satirical depiction of America.

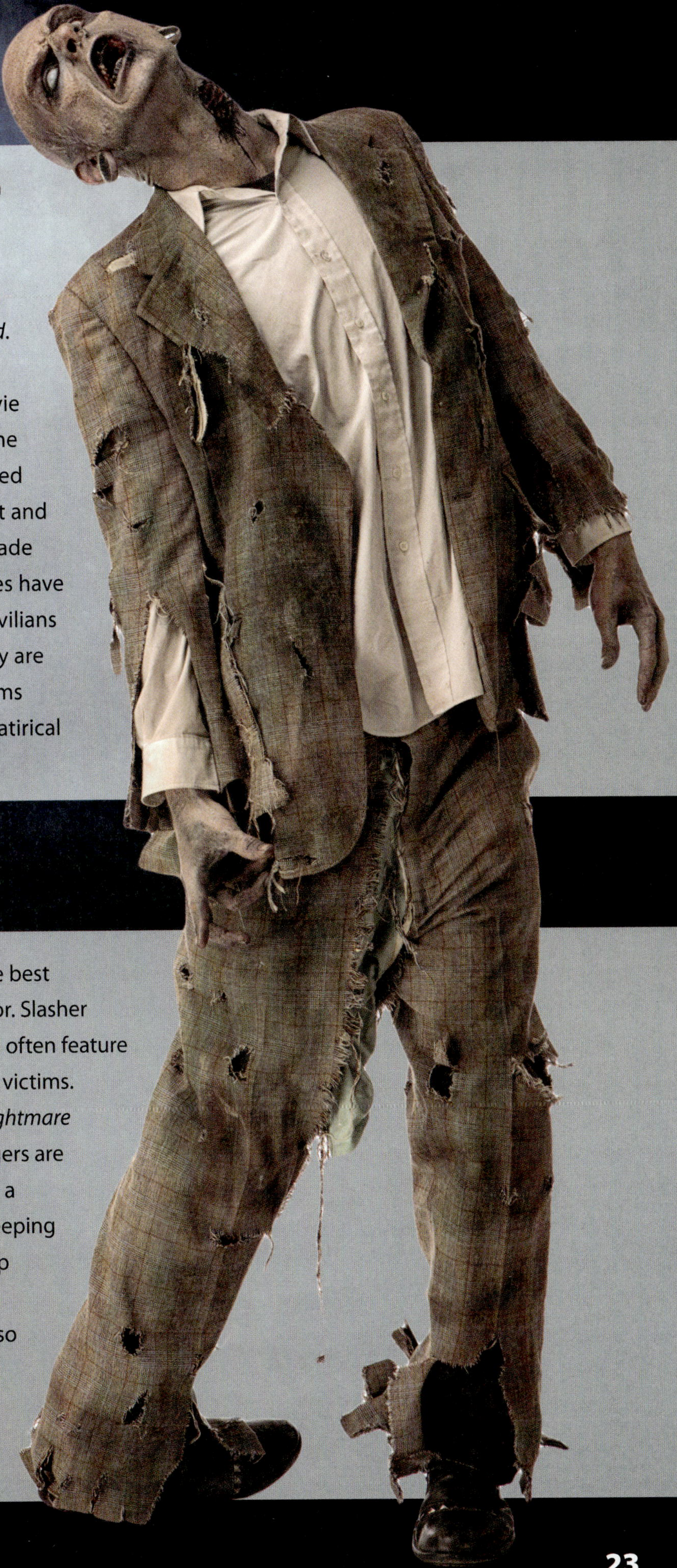

Wes Craven is considered one of the best filmmakers in the "slasher" genre of horror. Slasher films date back to Hitchcock's *Psycho* and often feature a mysterious or masked killer stalking his victims. Craven's most famous slasher film is *A Nightmare on Elm Street*. In this film, sleeping teenagers are hunted and murdered in their dreams by a character named Freddy Kreuger. The sleeping kids who are killed in their dreams end up dying in real life, and those around them are unable to understand why. Craven also directed the entire *Scream* movie series, which poked fun at some of the slasher films Craven had made popular.

Vincent Price: Master of Menace

by Velutha Paapen

Vincent Price was a famous American actor and narrator, known for playing the wicked villain in horror films and for his distinctive voice. Price was born in 1911 in St. Louis, Missouri. His father was president of a major candy company, and Price attended private school and later Yale University. He initially moved to London to study art in his twenties, but then fell in love with acting.

Though he became well known for his horror films, Price started out as a character actor. He had a tall build, thin frame, and unforgettable voice that made him perfect for parts that required a unique personality. Price soon found his calling as the villain in horror films, however. He starred in *House of Wax*, a wildly successful film that had Price playing an insane, disfigured artist who creates wax sculptures out of the bodies of his victims. *House of Wax* was one of the first movies filmed in 3D, and helped make Price known as the "Master of Menace."

Price was also well-known for his acting in *The Fly*. This horror movie was dark and terrifying as well as slightly comedic. In *The Fly*, Price plays the brother of a scientist. The scientist's experiments go terribly wrong, and he begins to transform into a fly. Price's character attempts first to save him, then to deal with his eventual murder. The rest of Price's acting career centered around horror films, including several movie versions of Edgar Allan Poe's writings, such as "The Raven."

Price was just as well known for his voice as he was for his acting. When he spoke, his words were precise, cultured, and expressive. He had the perfect, creaking voice for a villain. Price's characters would often break out into a terrifying, hysterical laugh, even as they were dying. In addition to acting, he did many narration and voiceover jobs. He hosted and starred in the radio program, *The Price of Fear*, gave voice to cartoon characters such as Professor Ratigan in *The Great Mouse Detective*, and delivered the opening lines for Michael Jackson's "Thriller."

Price narrated a film documentary on the artist Marc Chagall, which won an Oscar for best short subject of the year in 1963. And in 1991, Vincent Price was recognized for his Career Achievement by the Los Angeles Film Critics Association. After a long career, Price died in 1993. His talent and unique voice made him a star during his life, and he remains well respected today.

Ghosts on Stage:

by Benjamin Rannells

If you want to see a ghost, go to the theater! Many theaters around the world claim one or more ghosts as permanent residents—or at least frequent (if unverifiable) visitors. And it's not just audience members who say they've seen the unearthly apparitions; actors and actresses, stagehands and crew, cleaners, and even security guards have reported mysterious sightings and paranormal activity in theaters around the world.

What is it that makes theaters such welcoming places for tales of visitors from the beyond? Maybe it's all the drama—the heightened emotion, commotion, and excitement of show business. The stage is apparently the perfect place for a diva, alive or dead; There are many legends of ghosts of past performers haunting theaters, having died inside them in some tragic or untimely way. Other commonly reported ghosts are theater owners or directors—people who loved hanging around the stage so much they just couldn't tear themselves away, even in the afterlife.

The story of the ghost at the Princess Theatre in Melbourne, Australia is an excellent example of this strange phenomenon. In March of 1888, the famous baritone singer Frederick Baker (commonly known

Federici at the Princess Theatre

by his nickname "Federici") was performing at the Princess in the opera *Faust*. This tragedy unfolds as Dr. Faustus sells his soul to a devil named Mephistopheles. Federici sang the part of the devil. At the end of the opera, Mephistopheles descends back into the flames of hell, dragging Dr. Faustus along with him. On his way down into hell (via a trapdoor in the stage), Federici suffered a massive heart attack and died. But when the director told the rest of the cast the sad news, they were confused; according to them, Federici had been with them at the end of the opera, bowing to the audience.

Ever since that day, Federici's ghost has, reportedly, been in residence at the Princess, appearing as a glowing blue light, making odd noises, and causing accidents and equipment malfunctions. He most often appears in the theater's dress circle, wearing his 1880s best: a top hat and cloak. A sighting of the ghost is said to be good luck.

The legend of Federici's ghost is so powerful that on the opening night of each new performance, the theater management leaves an open seat for him.

That's all very well, but would you like to sit next to a ghost?

Teens and Terror: The Thrill of Horror Movies

by Mia Lewis

The first vampire movie, **Nosferatu,** *was released in 1922 and was based on the 1897 book* **Dracula** *by Bram Stoker.*

What's playing at your local multiplex? Chances are you'll find at least one horror movie starring zombies, aliens, demons, vampires, psycho killers, or killer creatures that are all expertly designed to scare you out of your wits. While some may think that sounds about as appealing as holding one's hand to a hot stove, the strange truth is that many people actually enjoy being scared silly. These horror enthusiasts are willing to pay good money to see a movie that will probably give them nightmares. The question is, why?

It Feels So Good When It's Over!

Compared to our caveman ancestors, most of us live pretty safe, predictable lives. It's natural to want to shake things up every once in a while. A horror movie is a good way to get the heart pumping and the adrenaline flowing without having to go hand-to-hand with a saber-toothed tiger.

Psychologists agree that people enjoy being scared when they know deep down that there's no real danger. A horror movie is a safe scare—one that will end when the lights come on. Besides, it feels so darn good when the movie is over; the stronger the fear and distress, the stronger the pleasure is when it stops. At the end of a horror movie, there's a sense of relief; you're finally putting that burned hand in ice water. Plus, you can feel proud and accomplished at having survived such terrors in one piece!

Over the decades, dozens and dozens of versions of Dracula-themed movies have been made.

Teens and Terror

Horror movies are especially appealing to teens and twenty-somethings. Again, the question is why? Generally speaking, teens and young adults seek out more stimulation and excitement than older adults. The younger folk are all about the thrills, chills, and adrenaline rushes, which is why they're into haunted houses and roller coasters, too. This urge dies down in older adults, as their need for thrills fades with age. In any case, older people are more likely to find real life is scary enough without any help from Hollywood.

For teens, another attraction of horror movies is that adults (OK, parents) probably don't approve. Seeing a horror movie is slightly transgressive, but at the same time it's safe, legal, and popular. It's a good way to be bad without being really bad.

Horror movies allow teens—especially boys—to practice and show off their mastery of fear. They might be afraid during the movie, but for the most part they don't run out screaming. Some psychologists say horror movies are a modern equivalent of tribal initiation into adulthood; watch a scary movie and you pass an unspoken test that grants you a membership into an exclusive club.

There are plenty of big scares on the small screen. Series such as "The Walking Dead," "Vampire Diaries," and "Teen Wolf," are notable.

(bg) ©Cristian Dina/iStockphoto.com; (t) ©Lightstar59/iStockphoto.com; (b) ©Lana K/Shutterstock

The horror genre has a vast history of low budget films offering B-level talent and cheap thrills. These movies may be a little less terrifying, as it is easier to tell that what's happening isn't real.

More Horrible Than Ever

The characters may be the same, but in other ways, the films made today are not your grandfather's horror movies. With computer-generated animation and other improved techniques, today's horror movies are much more realistic, and that makes them much scarier. Modern films are also gorier, more graphic, and more shocking. Directors are always trying to up the ante. As moviegoers get increasingly desensitized to every new shock and horror, the newest movies have to ratchet it up a notch, and another notch, and another. Some people hope this trend will begin to reverse itself when the audience's tolerance for terror and gore maxes out.

It's OK to Hate Horror

If you hate horror movies, don't worry, you're not alone. Many people don't like them, and for good reason. Horror movies have the potential to be psychologically searing. Just like with real traumatic events, our brains store the scary images from horror movies. These images are hard to erase; they can come back to disturb and scare us even years later. Again, the question is obvious: Why not avoid putting those haunting images in our heads in the first place?

So, don't feel shy about saying "no" if you don't feel like going to a horror movie with the rest of the gang. You might just be doing yourself a favor.

WHAT'S SCARY TO YOU?

Here are some potentially scary situations. Give points from 1–10, 10 being the scariest one. We left one blank, so you can include your idea of a scary situation, if you want!

☐ **You are home alone and you hear strange noises.**

☐ **There's a blackout and you have to come home alone in the evening.**

☐ **You are watching a movie with a scary doll or clown.**

☐ **Your friend, who was hiding, screams at you when you open the door.**

☐ **There's an earthquake and your whole house is shaking.**

☐ **You forgot about your math final test... and it is today!**

☐ **Your mom can't drive you to soccer practice, but your sister, who just got her license, can!**

☐ **You are ice-skating in a lake and hear a... crack!**

☐ **You are on a boat in the ocean and see a big storm approaching.**

☐ **You are swimming at the beach and you spot a dark fin near you!**

☐ ______________________________

The Move Toward FREEDOM

Women's Fashion, Women's Freedom

Open Air Zoos

Living Off the Grid

A Legendary Escape

Women's Fashion, *and* Women's Freedom

by Mia Lewis

Just look at the fancy ladies below. Imagine how many hours—and how many servants—it took to get them dressed! Today's women are too busy to wear outfits so time-consuming to put on, take off, and care for. Besides, those kinds of dresses would make it difficult to go to school, work, or exercise. Women nowadays don't allow their clothing to set limits on what they can and cannot do!

It was not so, one hundred years ago and more. Throughout many eras of history, women—especially wealthy women—wore elegant but impractical clothing that restricted their ability to move about freely. Women's role in society back then was, in most cases, extremely limited: They couldn't vote; they mostly didn't work outside the home; and they had little or no independent financial, legal, or social status, except as a daughter or wife. In other words, wealthy women's lives were as restricted and ornamental as their clothing.

Looking beautiful according to the latest fashion was the way to secure a husband, which at the time was women's most important mission. Women felt pressure to follow style rules, even when they were so extreme as to be downright dangerous. Several Western fashions right up to the end of the nineteenth century were harmful to women's health and safety—for example, corsets and crinolines.

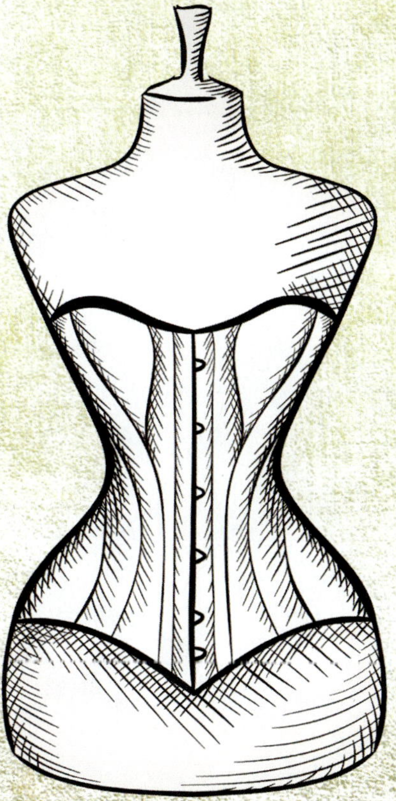

A **corset** is an undergarment designed to hold and shape the torso. It was made of flexile fabric stiffened with strips of hard material—often whale bone. Corset styles changed depending on what shape of torso was needed to go with what shape of dress. Tight-laced corsets were popular in the U.S. in the 1820s-1830s, and 1880s-1890s. These corsets created exaggerated hourglass figures and unnaturally tiny waists. Concerns over the negative effects of these corsets on women's health led to dress-reform movements and innovations such as "health corsets," which were looser and more flexible.

Crinolines were stiffened petticoats, rigid skirt-shaped structures that supported and shaped women's ever-wider skirts and dresses. Originally made of horsehair and linen, by the 1850s they were being constructed of steel hoops. Skirts this enormous led to all kinds of mishaps, some comic, some tragic. A lady in a large crinoline turning around in a china shop would knock everything off the shelves! When the wind caught the bottom edge, it flapped up like a sail; ladies took to wearing full-length undergarments to protect their modesty on windy days. But, when these dresses caught fire, the results were often deadly.

Cartoonists of the day enjoyed making fun of crinolines. While clearly impractical and excessive, they were actually liberating compared to the heavy petticoats of the previous era—lighter and more hygienic. The spring steel in a hoop skirt was flexible and could easily be compressed if a lady wanted to walk through a doorway or sit down. It just took a bit of practice to learn how to maneuver without knocking anything over or exposing your (long) underwear.

The 1890s to the 1920s were known as the **Progressive Era.** It was a time of swift and profound social transformation. Urbanization, industrialization, and mass immigration meant everything was changing: women's roles and fashions were no exception.

In the Progressive Era, women became more active and liberated—more were working, playing sports, actively participating in society, and demanding their rights, including the right to vote. Fashions reflected these changes. Women began to wear simpler and more practical outfits suitable for working in an office—as more young women were doing. Women's skirt suits imitated men's suits, as if to emphasize that they deserved the same rights and privileges.

The pace of change accelerated between 1910 and 1925. Hemlines rose, showing first a glimpse of ankle, then more and more of the lower leg; corsets loosened and then all but disappeared; dresses became less restrictive and more revealing. Women began to wear "step in" underwear instead of fuller, more elaborate layers. Some cut their hair into a short and stylish "bob"—impossible to imagine just a few years earlier.

In 1920, women won the right to vote. You can be sure that when these liberated women went to cast their ballots, they were dressed appropriately.

*The famous 1920s flapper dresses were all about **freedom:** freedom to move, think, act, and dance!*

From Cage to Forest:

Open-Air Zoos

by Casey Sullivan

Most people won't have the chance to ever see a grizzly bear eat a bushful of berries or a young orangutan use a leaf as an umbrella, at least not in the wild. But if you're one of the 175 million people who visit an American zoo each year, you might get to see animals do those very things. The nature of zoos, as well as the role they play, has changed a lot over the years.

The earliest predecessors of today's zoos were called "menageries," collections of exotic animals from across the world. The oldest known menagerie was in ancient Egypt, housing hippos, baboons, and elephants way back in 3500 BCE. Rulers— from ancient Babylon to the Kings of France—would collect foreign and eye-catching species the same way they collected gems or statues. Modern, public zoos with animals displayed for entertainment and education, first opened in London in 1847.

Early zoos weren't generally concerned about the physical and mental health of animals. Many creatures were confined to small cages, with little attention given to their needs. Confined in small quarters and without stimulation, many animals experienced great stress and also suffered from disease.

In the 20th century, zoos began to change. The San Diego Zoo was founded in 1916 and pioneered the idea of open-air zoos, cageless displays that resembled animals' native environments. Instead of being trapped behind bars, moats separated the animals from zoo visitors, keeping both safe with less confinement.

The San Diego Zoo's Monkey Trails exhibit is typical of an open-air zoo display. An old-style zoo would have had individual species in a display, but the open-air zoo mixes them together as they would be in the wild. The Lost Forest showcases animals, particularly

monkeys, from the rainforests of Asia and Africa. Native trees and vegetation are used to re-create a natural habitat. Monkeys like guenons and mandrills live together next to pygmy hippos, crocodiles, and Madagascar hissing cockroaches. Visitors observe animals interacting from above, on what's called the "Monkey Trails" in the treetops.

Over the years, zoos have started to play an important role in conservation. With more and more species at risk of extinction, zoos have begun focusing on maintaining populations of endangered species. The San Diego Zoo was essential in preventing the California condor from going extinct. California condors are the largest land birds in North America. They nest in cliffs and live in large groups. Disturbances from humans can easily prevent them from hunting or breeding. In 1987, not a single individual California condor was alive in the wild. The

species was virtually extinct, except for a few remaining condors in zoos. The San Diego Zoo began breeding its condors and helped reintroduce them to the wild. Today, there are more than 400 California condors. They are still at risk, but the conservation efforts of zoos have kept them from going extinct.

Zoos have also started protecting animals that live in the wild. New York City's Bronx Zoo, for example, is run by the Wildlife Conservation Society. The Society has 500 conservation projects all over the world, protecting 200 million acres of important habitat. The Society also works on issues that directly affect animals, such as illegal poaching, habitat restoration, and climate change.

As zoos work to better serve their animals, the environment, and the public, the nature of traditional zoos are changing. Some animal-welfare advocates argue that certain species can't easily be kept in captivity. Wild African Elephants, for example, live in complex family groups and can migrate across vast distances in search of food and water. Even the best zoos have a hard time replicating these conditions. Some, like Seattle's Woodland Park Zoo and the Bronx Zoo, have decided that they're better off retiring their elephant exhibits altogether. As time goes on, zoos will continue to change and evolve. From the private collections of ancient kings, to the open-air conservation organizations of today, zoos have changed a lot. What do you think they'll be like in the future?

©Domes/iStockphoto.com

There are many definitions of the word *freedom*. Here, the writer looks at a famous case of men seeking their physical freedom—from prison.

A Legendary Escape

by Matt Silvestri

Alcatraz is a small island in the middle of the San Francisco Bay. The main building on this island began as a fort and then became a military prison in the 1850s. About 70 years later, it became a Federal prison. Known as "The Rock," Alcatraz has housed some of America's most dangerous criminals, such as gangsters Al Capone, Mickey Cohen, and Whitey Bulger.

Today, Alcatraz is a very popular tourist attraction. But starting in 1934 until it closed as a prison in 1964, it was not a place you'd want to visit. The Rock was developed to be the first high-security federal prison in the country: a "maximum-security, minimum-privilege" jail for the worst convicts from around the country. In the 1920s and 30s, mob and gangster crime was widespread in the U.S., and Alcatraz was one way for the government to fight it. The plan was for the Rock to be "escape-proof." There were extra strong bars, constant surveillance, check-ins of prisoners up to twelve times a day, and ice-cold water and dangerous currents surrounding the island. Despite the difficulty, prisoners did attempt to escape. One famous escape was on June 11, 1962.

Frank Morris was no stranger to attempted escapes. He and his fellow prisoners, the brothers John and Clarence Anglin, were all non-violent bank robbers who were sent to Alcatraz because of their many attempts at escaping from other prisons. However, the isolated location and harsh Pacific waters did not deter them. In December, 1961, they joined forces with another prisoner, Allen West, and began working on their plan.

Clarence Anglin

The men realized that with a little ingenuity, they could craft tools using various items from around the prison. Using old saw blades and the motor from a broken vacuum cleaner, the men made drills that they used to loosen the air vents in their cells. They pierced the cover of the vents with closely spaced holes so that it could be removed. They managed to conceal their work with suitcases and pieces of cardboard.

John Anglin

A vacuum-cleaner motor

Using the vents, the men were able to access an unguarded area, which they used as their workstation. Slipping away before the final count for the night, with one man keeping watch, the four prisoners slowly created their tools for escape, including a raft and life vests crafted from more than 50 raincoats.

Frank Lee Morris

From the holes, the men climbed the pipe works more than 30 feet to the roof.

On June 11, 1962, the Anglin brothers and Morris put their plan into action. It's believed that Allen West was not ready, so he was left behind. After the final prisoner check-in of the night, the men got up and put dummy heads in their beds. They had concocted the real-looking heads out of soap and paper, using human hair taken from the prison barber shop. They opened their vents, went through the holes, and used pipes as a ladder up to a landing. Once there, they went through an air vent in the ceiling to the roof. The three ran across the roof, slid down an outdoor pipe, climbed over a fence, made their way down a staircase to a hillside, and finally reached the water.

A cell in the Federal Penitentiary at Alcatraz

On the morning of June 12, the dummy heads were discovered, and the prison went into high alert. The FBI was contacted to help with the investigation and search, but the three men could not be found, and ultimately never were. It's not known if the men escaped or died in the cold bay.

A courtyard in the Federal Penitentiary at Alcatraz

The odds were very much against Morris and the Anglin brothers, and most believe they died in the frigid water. But recent studies have shown that they actually could have survived if they left between eleven and twelve at night, when currents would have been favorable for reaching the shore. During any other time, the currents would have flowed too strongly in the wrong direction. Hypothermia would have set in before the men could reach safety.

Will we ever know? There was a legend that the men would return to the island 50 years after the day they disappeared. The Anglins' sister showed up just in case they did. So did U.S. marshals. But there was no sign of the three, and the mystery endures.

FREEDOM OF SPEECH QUIZ!

A phrase using the word *freedom* that you've probably heard a lot is *freedom of speech*. Do you know the history of this important freedom that people still fight for all over the world? See if you can answer the questions below, and then check your answers at the bottom of the page.

1. In 1791, freedom of speech was established in the First Amendment of the ______.
2. Greek philosopher ______ was prosecuted in 399 BCE for an early argument in favor of free speech.
3. The United Nations recognized free speech as a human right in 1948, in the ______.
4. Protection of speech was first introduced when the ______ was signed in 1215.
5. During the 1940s and 1950s, Senator ______ prosecuted people in the press, film, and television for favoring liberal ideas he considered anti-American.
6. ______ was condemned by the Inquisition after claiming that the sun does not revolve around the earth.
7. ______ wrote in favor of free speech in his book, *The Education of a Christian Prince*, in 1516.
8. In 1789, the ______, a fundamental document of the French Revolution, provides freedom of speech.

a. International Declaration of Human Rights
b. Magna Carta
c. Erasmus
d. Declaration of the Rights of Man
e. United States Constitution
f. McCarthy
g. Socrates
h. Galileo

ANSWERS: 1.e; 2.g; 3.a; 4.b; 5.f; 6.h; 7.c; 8.d

Approaching Adulthood

About Age ▪ Views on Adulthood
Careers ▪ Home or Away?

How Old Is
The Rights and Responsibilities

In the United States, it's commonly believed that age 18 signals adulthood. Eighteen-year-olds are afforded new rights and responsibilities, but there are still things they aren't legally allowed to do. Some would argue that we should gain all of our rights at one age, while others believe a gradual earning of rights is the best practice. This complicated issue hinges on the question: Is the age of adulthood the same as the age of responsibility?

All age-restricted laws operate on the principle that children aren't ready to make responsible choices or be held accountable for them—adults are. But how do we decide when childhood ends and adulthood begins? And why does this answer vary not just from country to country, but from law to law and state to state. In the United States, for example, some states allow you to drive at age 16. People can vote and enlist in the military at 18, and purchase alcohol at 21. At 18, you are legally responsible for your choices and actions. You are able to buy a house, sign a contract, take out a loan. But you can't rent a car or run for most political offices. Children much younger than 18, however, can be tried as adults for certain crimes. The age limits in this country are diverse and don't always make logical sense.

©Maridav/Shutterstock

Old Enough?

of Adulthood

by Amanda MacGregor

Age restrictions around the world also vary widely. They are generally tied to the social and cultural values of a society, as well as to convenience and tradition. Most countries allow citizens to vote at age 18, but in Malaysia and Kuwait that age is 21. In Argentina and Cuba, however, the voting age is 16. Marriageable age is generally 18 around the globe, but, interestingly, the ages often differ for males and females. In China, men must be at least 22 and women at least 20. In Bolivia, boys can get married at 16 and girls at 14 with parental permission. Military enlistment is at age 18 in a majority of countries, but can be as young as 16 or 17 with parental consent. The United States is in the minority of nations that allow 16-year-olds to drive—in most countries, you must be 18. Some countries allow children as young as 14 to drive with parental supervision.

There are many compelling arguments why the ages for different rights should vary. Becoming an adult is an ongoing process that doesn't happen all at once. The laws take into consideration the risks and benefits of allowing people of a certain age to participate in any given activity. Perhaps one of the most interesting arguments on why age matters comes from neuroscience. Our brains develop well into our twenties, particularly the part of our brain that helps with problem solving, decision making, and impulse control. Scientists who study adolescent brain development talk about "cold cognition" and "hot cognition." Cold cognition involves logic and sound judgment. A 16-year-old's cold cognition is as developed as an adult's. But hot cognition relies on emotion and peer pressure. It doesn't develop until ages 18 to 21. So scientific factors support a sliding age range for granting adult privileges—adolescents are simply not ready to make wise decisions. They tend to take risks and act impulsively. Their rash behavior could endanger their lives and the lives of others, and their decisions could have serious, long-lasting consequences. So an age restriction isn't so much about denying a right as it is about delaying a privilege until the brain is more fully developed.

On the other hand, many people feel that staggering these rights and setting what seem like arbitrary age limits is wrong. These people would argue that age shouldn't matter for precisely the same reasons—adulthood and maturity don't happen all at once and vary from individual to individual. Since the exact age of adulthood cannot be settled upon, why not just pick one age for everything and let people sort out what they feel ready to do? Society sends young adults mixed messages by having so many different ages for different responsibilities. The law cannot take into consideration every individual and how they may choose to use or abuse a right.

The issue of how old is old enough is complex and steeped in politics, tradition, culture, safety, science, and research. Laws will be obeyed, disregarded, or abused by people of all ages. The bottom line is that adulthood—regardless of when it occurs—is a process that comes with many responsibilities. The best we can hope is that young adults will make wise decisions as they encounter each new responsibility.

(t) ©Marta Paniti/Shutterstock; (b) ©oliveromg/Shutterstock

Adulthood: Different Views, Different Traditions

by Mandy Doherty

Each of us approaches adulthood in our own, unique way. Our family, classmates, and interests will all have an effect on the type of adult we become. Another major factor in our development is the culture in which we are raised. This can include our family's national and religious heritage and the neighborhood in which we grow up. There are many varying cultural views on what it means to become an adult. Let's take a look at some of these views and traditions.

Becoming Independent

In many American families, a large part of becoming an adult is developing a sense of independence and individuality. Eighteen is traditionally considered the age at which adulthood truly begins. For many people, this age coincides with graduation from high school and embarking on a new stage of life. Some pursue higher education, some seek out jobs, many move away from home and start out on their own.

Staying at Home

Remaining in the family home further into adulthood is part of the culture in southern Europe. This practice has even increased in recent years, due to economic reasons. However, this does not necessarily indicate a lack of independence in a young person, but instead a traditional belief in families remaining close together. In Italy, for example, a recent study showed that nearly four out of five young adults were living in the family house. Many of them move away only when they marry and start families of their own.

La Quinceañera

In many parts of Latin America, especially in North and Central America, a girl's transition to adulthood is celebrated with a quinceañera, a big party that acknowledges that the young woman is no longer a child. In Hispanic culture, there is also a wider acceptance of remaining in the family home during young adulthood.

Warrior Class

The Masai of Kenya and Tanzania celebrate the coming of age of their boys by initiating them into the "warrior class" of their tribe. After spending the night sleeping in the forest, they come back to a festivity that features dancing and singing. These young people will live in warrior camps for the next 10 years.

Ji Li, Guan Li, and Seijin-no-Hi

Japan and China also have coming of age festivities for their young people. In Japan, on the second Monday of January, girls who are 20 years old get to dress up in traditional clothing to celebrate Sejin-no-Hi. This marks that they are now contributing members of society. In some parts of China, there are ceremonies (Guan Li for boys and Ji Li for girls) to honor youth who are entering adulthood. In Ji Li, the young women begin to wear their hair in traditional buns.

An Inuit Tradition

Weather and survival skills are part of the coming of age for the Inuit in North Baffin Island. By the time a boy is 11 or 12, he has to pass a test of hunting skills and survival in the harsh weather, by going out into the wilderness with their fathers.

Modern Traditions

Many other cultures have their own traditional coming of age rituals—like sandanggu for Hindu girls, or the Sun Ceremony for young Apache girls—but some are slowly dying out, as more and more young people become influenced by the modern world. Rather than announcing to the world that they are ready to marry and start a family at an early age, youth today often prefer to pursue their education or professional career first.

(t) ©Dmitry Kalinovsky /Shutterstock; (b) ©Rido/Shutterstock

Planning Your Career:

What do you want to do and how will you get there?

by Casey Sullivan

You've probably been asked before what you want to be when you grow up, but have you put much thought into how you will get there? Taking time to think about and plan your career can help get you on the path to rewarding work later in life. Consider the type of work you want to do, the skills you have and those you will need to develop, and the lifestyle you see for yourself in the future.

A good career should satisfy multiple needs. If you're lucky, your career will reflect your interests and what you like to do. But, what if you aren't sure what your interests are, or what talents you have? Ask yourself: If you had your own TV show, what would it be about? What do you enjoy so much that you would want to share it with the world? This will help you focus on your passions.

Take Olivia. As a student, she was always interested in the outdoors. She loved hiking and camping and would tell her friends and classmates in vivid detail about her adventures. When she thought about her career, she wanted something that related to her love of nature and wilderness.

In high school, she interned in the city Parks Department, but found out it was a lot more office work than outdoor work. To get back out in the woods, she spent her summers working with a tour agency, guiding people on hikes and fishing trips. In college, she studied environmental science and focused on becoming an ecologist. Ecologists study the relationships between plants, animals, and the environment.

Olivia's daily tasks now include a lot of fieldwork, where she surveys and records species in the wild. This work can keep her outside for weeks at a time, camping on site. The rest of the time she does laboratory work, testing water and soil to see the impact of pollutants on wilderness. She loves her job, but would prefer a more regular work schedule and is considering training to become an environmental consultant.

Your career should utilize your skills and talents in a rewarding way. To identify your skills, ask yourself: What are the subjects or activities in which friends ask for your help? These are probably the ones in which you have the most skill. Identifying your talents can help you think about jobs in which you might be able to use them. For example, as a teen, Alberto was a smooth talker and a natural performer. When his friends needed someone to talk the teacher into pushing back a due date or to help them get out of trouble, they turned to him. Alberto looked for a career in which he could use his charisma in his work.

Alberto followed his talents and pursued a career in the entertainment industry. In high school, he participated in his school plays and in debate club, taking any opportunity to get on stage. Although he was never very successful as an actor, he eventually realized that he liked meeting people, making deals, and building relationships just as much as acting. He began to work in an entertainment agency.

Entertainment agents promote the careers and manage the business affairs of artists. They work to get auditions for their clients and negotiate their contracts. This job allows Alberto to harness his skills as a communicator and negotiator. The work requires him to be persuasive, confident, and persistent. As he gathers more clients and helps make their careers a success, he is even considering starting his own agency.

What do you want to be when you grow up?

Of course, your career should be rewarding, financially and emotionally. Depending on what motivates you, you might chose to follow a career path with high financial rewards or one that gives you plenty of free time. Consider, too, the amount of training you'll need for a career and how much that will cost. Do you want to spend years in school or get right out into the workforce? Your answer will help you choose the types of careers you might pursue.

As you begin to think about your future career, don't rely just on the stories of Olivia and Alberto or the experiences of your parents and family friends.

Reach out to people working in careers that interest you. An e-mail or letter to someone you admire asking them how they got ahead in their career can give you valuable insight. Most libraries will have career books describing various careers, their typical responsibilities, the skills and training required, and average salary. Test a career by volunteering or interning. But whatever you do, don't go into your working years blindly! Planning a career and exploring your options can help you secure rewarding and fulfilling work later in life.

Will You Stay or Will You Go?

by Lolo Lime

(c) ©Mariday/Shutterstock; (r) ©ssuaphotos/Shutterstock

One of the biggest decisions that comes with creating a plan for college is whether to move away from your family. There are multiple advantages and disadvantages you will have to consider before you can find the right answer for you.

When you move away from home, you lose some of the support that comes with being physically near your family. Our families often make us feel more secure and confident. Since your parents are invested in your well-being and care about your success, they can help you cope emotionally when you are struggling. On the other hand, living away from home gives you the opportunity to gain a different type of support through new friends and social circles. You will be surrounded by other students who can understand the transition you are going through.

Another thing to consider is the financial difference between living at home and on your own. Living at home may eliminate the need to pay rent or dorm fees. Many colleges even require the purchase of a meal plan for students living in dorms. Remaining with your family can certainly reduce the cost of groceries and other living expenses.

Living on your own during college can help you gain a level of independence that may not be achieved if you remain at home. Moving away helps you develop the confidence and self-sufficiency to take care of yourself and make your own informed decisions. When you're younger and living at home, your parents tend to be part of the decisions you make. When you're living on your own, you gain the experience to make wise choices for yourself.

College campuses often host many social and academic events. These can give you the chance to explore new interests and discover new passions: opportunities you might not come across if you remain at home. Many consider the broadening of their horizons to be a large part of the college experience. Having the chance to figure out what topics and activities you care most about can help you make the best decision about which major is the right one for you.

Some students, however, see these social events as a distraction from their studies. Living at home can remove these types of distractions and provide you with a place to go where you can focus more fully on your studies.

Thinking about all these considerations is important as you create a plan for your future. Be sure you're ready!

AS YOU GROW UP . . .

What things are you looking forward to the most as you grow up? Order them from 1 to 10 (1 being the thing you just can't wait to do). You may not want to do everything on the list . . . and that's ok!

☐ **Get a driver's license.**

☐ **Vote.**

☐ **Travel on your own.**

☐ **Go away for college.**

☐ **Get married.**

☐ **Have a child.**

☐ **Rent a house/apartment with friends or roommates.**

☐ **Get your own house or apartment.**

☐ **Start your own business.**

Personal Legacy

Isaac Newton's Mind

Stan Lee's Comic Books

Neil deGrasse Tyson's Cosmos

Bob Dylan's Music

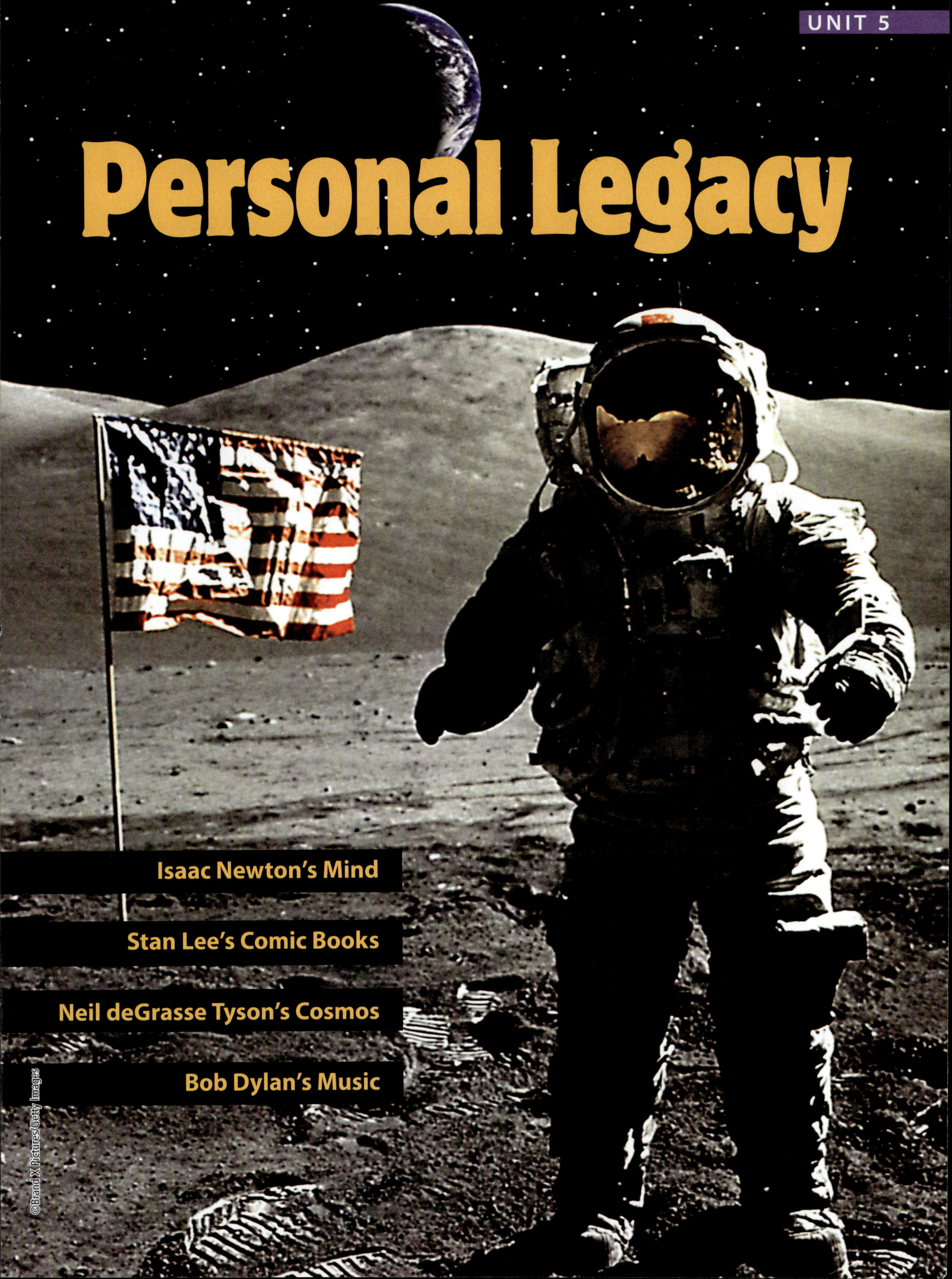

When Inspiration Grows on Trees

by Mariam Suri

One name always comes up when scientists, astronomers, and mathematicians are asked to name the smartest people who ever lived: Sir Isaac Newton.

Achievements by the Age of 26

Laws of Motion Newton discovered the three laws that govern the effects of force on an object's motion.

Gravity Newton discovered that there is a gravitational force between any two objects in the universe, depending on their masses and the distance between them.

Light Spectrum Newton discovered that white light is made up of all the colors. (He divided the spectrum into red, orange, yellow, green, blue, indigo, and violet.)

Reflecting Telescope Newton invented a telescope that used mirrors to reflect light and form an image.

Calculus Newton invented a branch of mathematics that is essential in the study and application of physics.

Newton's light spectrum disk

The story that most people have heard about Newton is that he discovered gravity when an apple fell on his head. Like most stories, it's only partly true.

Newton made lengthy studies of the orbit of the moon. He had finally realized that the same force that made objects fall toward the ground had an effect over very long distances. This led to his mathematical formula that calculated how much gravitational force decreases with distance.

But what about the apple? There are documents from the era that shed some light on the story. William Stukely wrote the first biography of Newton. Even though Newton was irritable and disagreeable, Stukley met with him frequently. One evening, the two were drinking tea outdoors—as English people do! They were under the shade of an apple tree. Stukely wrote that Newton remarked that the situation was the same as when he had first thought about gravity. Newton remembered wondering why an apple always fell perpendicularly to the ground, but never sideways. He realized that the apple was attracted to the center of the earth. Why? The earth concentrated the force at its center, and the earth's matter was attracting the matter of the apple. If matter attracted matter, he concluded, then the apple must also apply a force to the earth. The force depended on the apple's mass.

Did You Know . . . ? Issac Newton

- He was born prematurely and was not expected to survive.
- Allegedly, he was a stutterer.
- His mother wanted him to be a farmer.
- He studied to get a law degree.
- He had the reputation of being an avid list-maker.
- He was a very quiet politician. As a member of Parliament for a year, rumor has it he only spoke once—to tell someone to close the window.
- After suffering a nervous breakdown in his later years, he became known for his eccentricities.
- His dog set his lab on fire and ruined 20 years of research.
- After his death, in 1727, at age eighty-five, much of his work was considered unsuitable for publishing.

Another account of a conversation with Newton was given by his niece's husband, John Conduitt. He reported that Newton recalled being in his mother's garden when he realized that the power of gravity wasn't limited to short distances.

So maybe apples did change the future of science. Unfortunately, there is no solid evidence that one actually fell on Newton's head. In any case, it was a great scientist, not a piece of fruit that did all the work. But in spite of Newton's remarkable genius, he gave credit to the scientists of the past:

"If I have seen further than others, it is by standing upon the shoulders of giants."

TRATADO
DE
ANÁLISIS
DE LOS
ANÁLISIS
POR
ECUACIONES

(bg) ©Gary Paul Lewis/Shutterstock; (l) ©s_bukley/Shutterstock.com

Stan Lee: Creator of Superheroes

by Casey Sullivan

If you've watched a movie, read a comic book, or seen a cartoon in the past few years, you've probably been exposed to the legacy of Stan Lee. As creator and editor of many comics and as president and chairman of one of the most famous comic book publishers, Stan Lee created some of the most popular and long-lasting superheroes of the last hundred years, including Spider-Man, the X-Men, the Hulk, the Fantastic Four, and others. Not only did Stan Lee help create influential characters, he also changed the way readers viewed them. His use of flawed and realistic superheroes helped comics evolve from a genre mostly targeted at children to an art form worthy of serious attention.

Stan Lee was born Stanley Martin Lieber, in New York City in 1922. His parents were Jewish immigrants from Romania who had traveled across the Atlantic to escape discrimination and find greater opportunity. As a child, he wanted to be a great writer. He made extra money writing obituaries and press releases. In 1939, Stan's uncle got him a job at Timely Comics, which eventually became Marvel Comics, the company he would one day lead. But at the time, Stan's major responsibility was to make sure that the artists didn't run out of ink.

Two years after he started, Stan was given the opportunity to write for an issue of Captain America. He signed his work with "Stan Lee" instead of his given name of Stanley Lieber. This play on his birth name became his pen name, or nom de plume, which is an assumed name authors use to hide their identity. Like many of his superheroes, Stan Lee had a secret identity.

At 19, Stan Lee became an editor. That was a pretty fast ascent for a young writer who had begun working in comics two years earlier and was just barely out of high school. Despite his quick success, neither Stan nor anyone he worked with could have guessed how important he would become. Stan spent the next twenty years writing comics in a variety of genres, from romances and science fiction, to Westerns and murder mysteries. He was good at it, but not great, and almost gave up on comics altogether.

Then, in the late 1950s, Stan Lee was assigned the task of reviving superhero comics. Superheroes like Superman and Batman had fallen out of fashion. They tended to follow a predictable pattern: they had a secret identity, a tragic background, extraordinary powers, and simple enemies. These heroes rarely had the problems of everyday people. They were never grumpy, lazy, or confused. This changed once Stan Lee got involved. His superheroes were much more human. They had stupendous powers, but also had bad tempers, were vain, or worried about what their girlfriends thought of them. These superheroes were extraordinary but normal in many ways, allowing readers to identify with them more easily than in past comics.

Stan Lee's first superhero creation, with his partner Jack Kirby, was the Fantastic Four. Together, these four superheroes fought evil but also bickered with each other the way siblings might. They became popular immediately. Lee and Kirby next created the Hulk, a shy scientist who morphs into a giant beast when overcome by anger or stress. The Hulk wasn't just a fighter of crime, but a metaphor for how rage can take over someone's actions and life.

Lee went on to create many more famous comic franchises, including Iron Man, Thor, and the X-Men. His characters redefined what it meant to be a superhero, and his comics began to address issues from the real world as well. Under Stan Lee, the comics started to include issues such as racism, discrimination, and drug use. These were topics once thought too serious for something like a comic book.

In 1972, over thirty years after he started working in the industry, Stan Lee stopped writing and became publisher of the company; he'd gone from replacing artists' ink to running the entire show. Stan Lee's legacy has continued to grow over the years. Today superheroes have the same realistic, complicated characteristics Stan first introduced. Many of his works have been turned into blockbuster movies. The Stan Lee Foundation continues his legacy, promoting literacy, education, and the arts. In 2008, the U.S. Congress awarded him the National Medal of Arts, placing him in the ranks of great artists such as painter Georgia O'Keefe, architect I. M. Pei, and actor James Earl Jones.

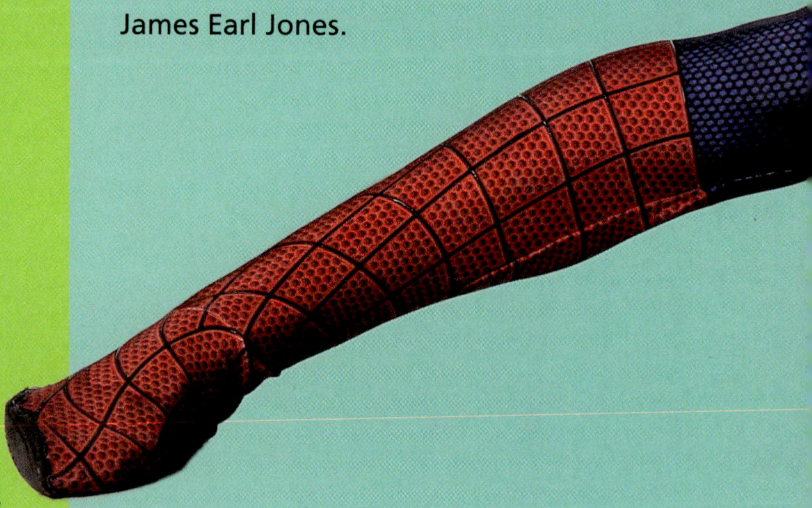

POW!
BOOM!
BAM

Neil deGrasse Tyson Brings Us the Cosmos

by Mia Lewis

Tyson's parents bought him his first telescope. Now he could see things he had only read about.

Astrophysicist Neil deGrasse Tyson had a life-changing experience at New York City's Hayden Planetarium when he was just nine years old. "It's just another museum until they turn out the lights and *the stars come out*," he said. Born and raised in the city, Tyson had never before seen so many or such bright stars. He was fascinated and amazed.

A few years later, Tyson's parents bought him his first telescope. Now he could see things he had only read about—craters on the surface of the moon; rings around Saturn.

And that's exactly what he became. Fittingly enough, after completing his PhD, one of his first jobs was at the Hayden Planetarium. Tyson's academic research included such topics as star formation, exploding stars, dwarf galaxies, and the structure of the Milky Way. He has published a dozen books, written numerous magazine articles, and served on important presidential commissions. He has an impressive stack of awards and honorary degrees and is a popular public speaker. He is currently the Director of the Hayden Planetarium—the place where it all started.

Today, Tyson is one of America's best-known and most beloved scientists. The wider public has gotten to know him through his many appearances on television. He hosted PBS's *NOVA ScienceNow* for several years and the hugely successful *Cosmos: A Spacetime Odyssey*. (*Cosmos* appeared in 181 countries, in 45 languages.) He appears regularly as a science expert on all kinds of television shows, weighing in on topics ranging from climate change to the importance of space exploration. His special gift is that he can explain difficult concepts to ordinary people without being condescending or confusing.

The other quality that makes Tyson so engaging is his endless wonder and enthusiasm for everything about astrophysics—the planets and stars, black holes, galaxies, the whole cosmos—and all science. It's hard to be bored when someone that *pumped* is talking about something they care about so much. For Tyson, science is about staying curious, and making the world a better place.

Bob Dylan, Songwriter for the "Now"

by Jarrod Zayas

©Express Newspapers/Stringer/Getty Images

The 1960s were a scary time in America. War raged in Vietnam, and many young Americans had to go there and fight. Images of the war made their way to the U.S. The news on TV made it feel like the war was happening in our own backyards. America also became a battleground as the civil rights movement erupted in the South. African Americans joined together in non-violent protest, seeking the same rights as whites. The violent backlash of those opposed to desegregation also flashed by on TV screens. How could a country founded on peace and freedom suddenly be filled with such unrest?

With so many voices shouting to be heard at the same time, who could speak for us all? Who would be the voice of this angry generation? The surprising answer came in the form of a young songwriter from Minnesota. His name was Robert Zimmerman. You may know him as Bob Dylan.

Corner of Commerce and Barrow Street in Greenwhich Village, Manhattan, NYC

Robert Allen Zimmerman was born in Duluth, Minnesota, on May 24th, 1941. The introduction of rock-and-roll music in 1955 heavily influenced young Robert. The fearless growl of Johnny Cash, the reckless piano playing of Little Richard, and the defiant way Elvis Presley danced on television all had a strong influence on him. He spent hours studying music coming from the radio and imitating it. He formed many bands while in high school. In his yearbook, Robert's classmates said that he might even join Little Richard's band in the future.

However, young Robert Zimmerman was unhappy. Rock-and-roll music was fun and it made you want to dance. But, the songs didn't really reflect Robert's life and the way that he felt. Where was the music about the troubled world? Where were the songs about the difficult feelings inside him? Robert realized that the American folk-music scene encouraged more honest songwriting. So Robert decided to make a big change. He began writing folk songs instead of rock and roll. Inspired by Dylan Thomas, one of his favorite authors, he went so far as to change his name to Bob Dylan.

Bob Dylan moved to New York City in January of 1961. Like many folk singers of the time,

©Fred W. McDarrah/Contributor/Getty Images

he played guitar and sang songs at many different clubs in Greenwich Village. With so many other folk singers performing in the same place at the same time, how did Bob Dylan manage to stand out? Perhaps it was his distinctive voice, which one popular author at the time compared to singing sandpaper. While it may not be the most beautiful voice you've ever heard, it sounds more real, more honest than voices of other singers. When Bob Dylan sings a song, you can really hear the journey he has taken.

Or perhaps Bob Dylan's music stood out from other singers because the songs he wrote were truly poetry. When he wrote about love or the unrest in the world around him, it was like he was writing for all of us. *Blowin' in the Wind*, a song Dylan wrote about war and freedom, was covered by some of the most popular artists of the time and became an anthem for the civil rights movement.

In the mid-1960's, Bob Dylan began to create music that didn't easily fit into the folk-music scene. His album *Bringing It All Back Home* featured electric instruments, replacing the acoustic guitar and harmonica that had been the staples of his signature sound. Many of his fans were angry, but Bob Dylan refused to make music that only satisfied his fans. The world was changing, and his heroes and influences were changing, too.

It was during this time that Bob Dylan recorded some of his most famous songs, including *Like A Rolling Stone* and *Sad-Eyed Lady of the Lowlands*. Bob Dylan was creating music that was more relevant than ever. His lyrics were heavily influenced by the beat poetry of the day. The new songs were lengthier than popular songs released at the time, and they highlighted not only his personal struggles, but also the continuing struggle of a swiftly changing America

Bob Dylan is now considered one of the most influential singer-songwriters of all time, consistently making music since the 1960s. He has won many awards and received the Presidential Medal of Freedom from President Barack Obama. Although his music sounds have changed over time, one thing remains true: Bob Dylan writes music for the now. His words and his "singing sandpaper" voice challenge us to look within ourselves to change the world. He is a true hero of the music industry and, indeed, of the world.

Dylan in Sheridan Square,
Greenwich Village, Manhattan, NYC

Who Did It?

1 Participated in the civil rights movement with his songs

2 Formulated the laws of gravity

3 Wrote influential books on astronomy

4 Created famous comic-book characters

Neil DeGrasse Tyson

Stan Lee

Bob Dylan

Isaac Newton

ANSWERS: 1. Bob Dylan; 2. Isaac Newton; 3. Neil DeGrasse Tyson; 4. Stan Lee

The Value of Work

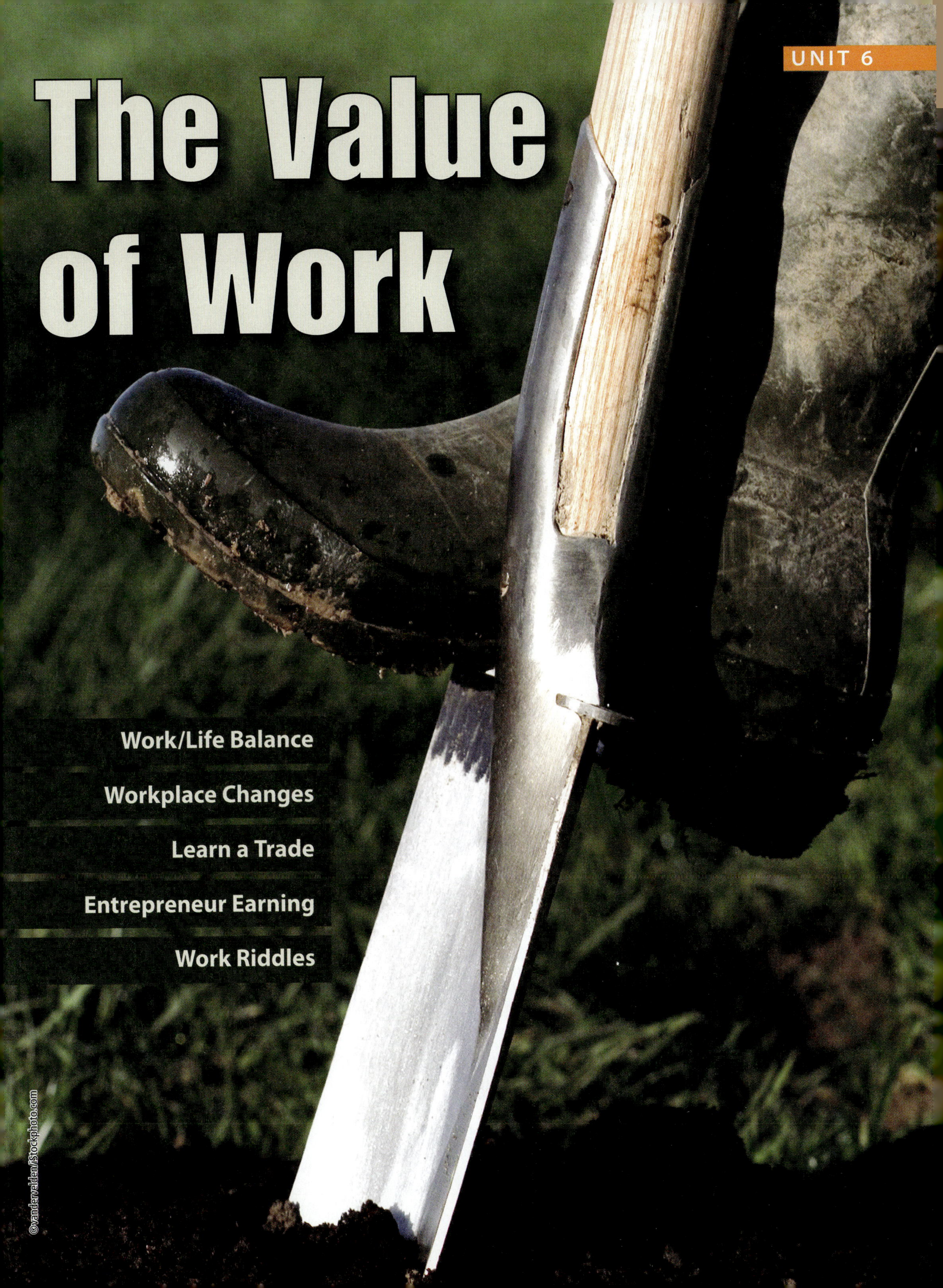

Work/Life Balance

Workplace Changes

Learn a Trade

Entrepreneur Earning

Work Riddles

How to Balance Work

BALANCING WORK AND LIFE

means doing your job well and enjoying yourself outside of work, too. When you work, you want to achieve certain goals, while still having things you want to do in your free time as well. How can you find a way to spend the right amount of energy on each part of your day?

Right now, your job is school. If you can learn to balance school and life as a student, when you have a career as an adult you can continue to have this balance. Planning your time, being healthy, and monitoring your time spent online and on your mobile devices are all important in maintaining balance.

Plan Your Time

Schedule a time of day for homework and for studying. Ideally, this time frame should be when you get home from school. Wait to answer those texts, tweets, and e-mails until after the work is done. You'll find that you won't need as much time to study, and that homework doesn't have to take over your life. Cutting down on outside distractions maximizes your study time. You will be working smarter, not harder!

Plan, also, for doing things you enjoy. Which afterschool activities do you want to be involved in? Do you want to play sports, work on the school newspaper, or join the science club? Can you find the time to do all of these things, or do you need to pick just a few that you can fit in?

Hang out with people who make you happy. Make time to go out with your friends and spend some relaxing time at home with your family.

and Life

Stay Healthy

Don't forget to exercise! If you play a sport, you know that physical activity can give you energy and help you think more clearly. If you're busy with other afterschool endeavors, how can you find time to stay active? Try walking or riding your bike when you go places, or take a run in your neighborhood after you finish your homework. It's always good to find a partner to exercise with, so that both of you stay motivated.

Try not to eat junk food while you're doing homework. Healthy snacks like fruit and nuts will help you stay alert. Eating too many sugary foods and drinks will make you crash!

Watch Those Devices

Since we turn to the internet for everything from researching a school project to organizing a day with friends, it can be difficult to tell the difference between work and recreational use. Pay attention to how your use your devices. When you do research, don't skip over to your email or favorite sites. Once you finish what you have to do, reward yourself with some time to reconnect with friends or to browse.

Try this three-pronged plan to balance your work and life. You may find you have more free time than you ever imagined!

(t) ©Mike Flippo/Shutterstock; (b) ©Jupiterimages/Polka Dot/Alamy

The Changing American Workplace

by Susan Markowitz Meredith

America's labor force is over 155 million workers strong. By 2020, its numbers will surpass 164 million—an enormous number of men and women in the workplace. By comparison, around 200 years ago, the American labor force held only two million people.

Our country's work force has changed not only in size, but also in the types of jobs most people have today, which are different from those in the past. About 60 percent of present-day workers are employed in white-collar occupations, compared to just 20 percent in 1900. An even greater transformation has occurred in agriculture. Whereas farm workers made up 40 percent of the labor force in the early 1900s, today's statistics are down to 1.5 percent. Job-market shifts like these are not unusual, though. The world of work is always changing, as scientific and technological advancements lead to the creation of new jobs and the elimination of others. Our information-technology-based economy has sped up this cycle to an even greater degree. To succeed, workers—and the companies that employ them—must be able and willing to adapt.

A good male-female balance

The 9-to-5 work world still exists, but alongside it are workplaces that offer employees more flexible hours. This adjustment to workers' schedules began to appear in the 1960s, when large numbers of women entered the labor force. Many mothers with children under the age of 18 needed to meet their responsibilities both at work and home.

The number of mothers in the workplace has steadily increased since 1975, when it was less than 50 percent, to around 78 percent today. So, it's no surprise that flexible scheduling has become an important issue for a growing number of workers. Many workers are women in two-parent households, and many others are single parents. Still others are fathers playing a more active role in their children's caregiving. Understandably, more American companies are creating policies to address their employees' work/life balance issues.

Diversity is a characteristic of American workplaces today. Whether someone is a healthcare practitioner or engineer, teacher or sales person, researcher or computer technician, his or her workplace consists of males and females working side-by-side. This fact is not surprising, as women make up nearly 50 percent of the labor force. Some predict that women workers will even exceed men by the year 2020. A look back to 1950 tells a different story, though, when just 29.6 percent of workers were women. Shifts in social attitudes, lower birth rates, and additional white-collar jobs brought about the enormous changes we see today.

In addition to the levelling out of men and women in the workplace, there are also more people of color—about 20 percent. Our workplace includes Hispanic, African American, Asian American, and other minority workers. These numbers in the labor force will likely increase as population groups change. Specifically, census data points to 2050 as the date by which the U.S. will officially have no ethnic or racial majority.

A third sign of diversity in today's workplace is the age difference among workers. In some companies, the age range spans more than 50 years. The youngest generation consists of recent graduates in their early twenties, while veteran employees are in their seventies. Everyone benefits in recognizing the unique perspective that comes from collaborating with different age groups.

This flexibility in the workplace has expanded well beyond scheduling for some American workers, who now perform their jobs from home on both a full-time and part-time basis. The dot-com boom of the 1990s started this phenomenon with the emergence of portable computers, the internet, and other advanced technologies. Today, telecommuting is more doable than ever. Of course, not every occupation or employee is suited to such a lifestyle, but when the match is good, remote workers thrive.

Being Your Own Boss

Instead of entering a pre-existing workplace as an employee, many young Americans are choosing to start their own businesses. They know that being an entrepreneur is a risky endeavor with no guarantee of profits. Still, according to many successful business owners, it's worth the effort. They remind newcomers, though, that turning a dream into reality requires a lot of hard work over a long period of time. The dream of having a great idea and suddenly making billions of dollars from it is highly unrealistic. Instead, hopeful entrepreneurs should set concrete goals regarding the products or services they want to offer, followed by a step-by-step process to reach those goals.

In today's high-tech world, it's easier than ever to start a small business. For instance, a low-budget option is to run a virtual office from your home without having to rent outside office space. Another method is to create your own website and use social media to make connections. While waiting for the business to start making a profit—which often takes months or even years—you can always opt to take a part-time or full-time job.

(t) ©Photodisc/Getty Images; (b) ©AVAVA/Shutterstock

Learning the TRADE

by Casey Sullivan

Exactly what does it take to be a plumber, mechanic, biologist, or lawyer? How do professionals learn their crafts? Through education, of course. Lawyers go to law school, doctors to medical school, etc. But not all professional learning takes place in a classroom. There are plenty of hands-on opportunities for people who want to start a career, or just to find out whether or not a job suits them.

(t) ©auremar/Shutterstock; (b) ©SOMKKU/Shutterstock

One of the best ways to get direct experience in a trade is through an internship or apprenticeship. An internship is an on-the-job training and education program for professional careers. Interns can be high school or college students, or just working people looking for new skills or for a career change. Generally, interns stay for a short time with a particular employer, learning the skills needed for a job by working with and around the professionals that do it. Some internships pay their interns, but many are unpaid, or for credit only.

A good internship combines fulfilling work with education. For example, a high school student might intern with a local architecture firm to learn what working as an architect entails. She definitely won't be able to plan or design buildings, because she won't yet have that kind of traning. However, her duties should still be worthwhile. Perhaps she will scout building sites, send emails to clients, or research local construction laws. She might sit in on meetings to get a taste of the way architects conduct business with one another. If she has a good internship, the student will get direct education from her supervisors. A managing architect might teach her how to use a design program or explain the reasoning behind a building's layout. When her internship ends, the intern will be able to take the skills she's gained and use them in her future career and education.

Besides being educational, internships can be used to develop important professional connections. A supervisor might think an intern is particularly impressive and write him a letter of recommendation for a job or college. Or, a boss might recognize that her intern was exceptionally good at a certain task and let him know when a job opportunity opens up. Internships can provide an important "foot in the door," as a lead into a new career.

Hands-on learning can also come in the form of an apprenticeship. Like an internship, an apprenticeship supplies on-site training in a particular skill. However, apprenticeships tend to be longer and require more hours. Unlike an internship, which you might do in the summer or for a few hours a week while in school, an apprenticeship is a full-time paid job that can last years. Another difference is that once you finish an apprenticeship, you are often certified to work in that field professionally. When you complete a plumbing apprenticeship, you can be a plumber right away, whereas interns require more training before they can start as professionals.

Since apprenticeships include most of a worker's professional training, they are often more focused on trades. Internships tend to focus more on professions. What is the difference? A trade typically involves working directly with your hands, such as in construction, carpentry, or farm work. By contrast, a profession usually involves more knowledge-based work, such as accounting, scientific research, or law. Professional work usually requires an advanced degree, while a trade can often be obtained through an apprenticeship alone.

Long before college educations were common, most people started their careers as apprentences. Today, the construction industry is the heaviest user of apprenticeship programs. An apprentice will typically work three to six years under an established program. For example, an apprentice working to be an electrician traditionally begins by observing the electrician's work, listening to his explanations, and assisting at basic tasks. A few hours of class often accompanies this. As the apprentice becomes more familiar, she begins doing more difficult tasks, under the supervision of a professional. Over the

years, she will have learned and done enough that she can eventually practice the trade on her own and begin her career as an independent electrician.

If you are considering pursuing a particular line of work, an internship can offer you valuable exposure and help you determine what work you enjoy and excel at. If you are looking to develop a trade and learn a skill, an apprenticeship can help you get the necessary experience. While an apprenticeship might seem like a major commitment compared to an internship, job shadowing and part-time work can also give you valuable exposure to a trade. Dabbling in many types of work can help you find the best career fit for you.

Earning Extra Cash:

If you've been earning an allowance since you were a kid, you know how nice it can be to have pocket money. But since you've gotten older, you may have started thinking about having a little more money. Sure, allowances are great for keeping your piggy bank full and providing you with some spending money. But videogames and weekend trips to the mall are expensive, and sometimes allowances just aren't enough.

If you think you could use some extra spending money, or if you just want to start saving up, it might be time to think about getting a job. Getting a job isn't always easy for teenagers, but it's not impossible. In fact, there are lots of ways you can use your skills and interests to start making some extra cash.

One of the best avenues into moneymaking is to become an entrepreneur. Although being an entrepreneur requires a lot of hard work, getting started is actually pretty simple. When it comes to making your own money, it all comes down to one easy recipe: Know your skills, be creative, spread the word, and stay organized.

Be an Entrepreneur

Tips for the Entrepreneur

1 **Know Your Skills:** Do you already earn an allowance from your parents for doing yard work? Walking the dog? Babysitting your younger siblings? If so, you already have the *required skills* to start doing similar work for others. When you're listing your skills, remember to also pay attention to things you enjoy doing, in addition to things you simply know how to do. For example, if you like reading, or practicing equations for math class, you can turn those interests into extra cash by tutoring younger kids, or even your friends. When you're trying to become an entrepreneur, your interests are just as important as your skills.

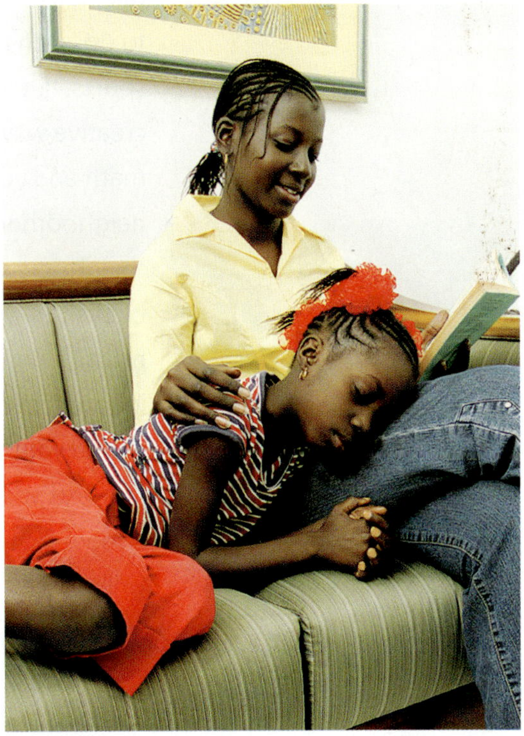

2 **Get Creative:** Once you know your skills and interests, you can be creatively combine them to make money. This can be hard, but if you start making lists, it's easier! First, make a list of all the things you know you can do, like walking dogs, babysitting, or raking leaves. Second, make a list of things you like to do, such as math, animals, reading, and playing sports. Put these lists next to each other and find a creative way to combine them. For example, if you like math and you can babysit, you can offer to work as a neighborhood babysitter who can also help kids with their homework. If you like animals and you're a good babysitter, you can put those skills together to be your neighborhood's pet-sitter. You could even fuse your love for sports with your babysitting skills and manage a local youth sports team. Combining your skills and interests will make you a *dynamic* worker, which makes it more likely that people besides your parents will be willing to pay for your services. Offering many skills might even allow you to raise your rates!

3 **Spread the Word:** Once you've found a perfect combination of skills and interests, you'll have to get the word out about the services you can offer. Consider posting flyers around your neighborhood or in local stores, listing your skills and the jobs you can do. You should also ask your parents to tell their friends that you're available to work. You could even put an ad in a school or church newsletter. No matter how you choose to spread the word, keep your personal information private until you're sure you can trust your future employers.

4 **Stay Organized:** This is important! After someone hires you, keep track of that person's name and contact information so that you can list them as a *reference*. A reference is someone who can recommend you for future jobs. You should also write down the skills you used and the skills you learned at your first few jobs. This strategy will get you started on an important list of your work history and skills called a *resume*.

Following these four steps will help get you to where you need to be to earn money as an entrepreneur. Besides, being a teenage entrepreneur also gives you important work experience that will make it easier for you to apply for other jobs in the future. Plus, a work history that shows your hard-working attitude might qualify you for a higher-paying summer job as a lifeguard or camp counselor, since these positions involve more responsibility and and may require previous work experience. So, whether you need extra money or just want to be prepared for the future, it's never too early to start thinking about jobs you can do. You have lots of options, so get out there!

RIDDLES about WORK

See if you can solve these riddles! Turn over the magazine to find the answers at the bottom of the page, then challenge your friends and family!

1 Why did the waiter stomp on the client's burger?

2 What is the difference between a composer and a letter carrier?

3 What kind of policemen enjoy their work the most?

4 What do you have to know to be a real estate salesperson?

5 What does a farmer grow if he works hard enough?

6 How is a judge like an English teacher?

ANSWERS: 1. Because the client was in a hurry and asked him to step on it! 2. The composer writes notes and the carrier delivers them. 3. The traffic policemen, because they whistle while they work. 4. Lots! 5. Tired. 6. They both hand out long sentences.